# Bassin' with a Fly Rod

# Bassin' with a Fly Rod

**One Fly Rodder's Approach
to Serious Bass Fishing**

by
**Jack Ellis**

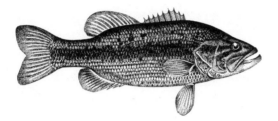

*Illustrations and cover design by Larry Largay*

Mountain Pond Publishing
North Conway, New Hampshire

Also by Jack Ellis:
*The Sunfishes*

Published by:
Mountain Pond Publishing Corp.
P. O. Box 797
North Conway, New Hampshire 03860
USA

Distributed by:
Lyons & Burford
31 West 21 Street
New York, NY 10010
USA

First Edition

Printed in the United States of America

Library of Congress Cataloging-in-Publication Data
Ellis, Jack, 1936 -
    Bassin' with a fly rod : one fly rodder's approach to
serious bass fishing / by Jack Ellis ; illustrations and cover
design by Larry Largay.
        p.   cm.
    Includes bibliographical references.
    ISBN 0-936644-21-4 (hbk.)
    1. Bass fishing -- Southern States. 2. Fly Fishing --
Southern States.        I. Title
SH681.E46    1995
799.1 ' 758 -- dc20                            94-38934
                    ⩗                          CIP

To James
Friend, sportsman, gentleman

# CONTENTS

# FOREWORD

Jack Ellis and I became aquainted through his seminal magazine articles when I was editor and publisher
of *American Angler* magazine. I enjoyed Jack's original
and thought-provoking writing, so when he asked me
to write a foreward to his upcoming book I was happy
to agree. At that time little did I know that I was also
to become involved in the book's publication—but it
really presents no problem because this book stands
by itself.

    *Bassin' With a Fly Rod* is more than a "how-to"
book, although most fishermen can gain much practical information from it's pages. It's a book about the
origins, the tradition, the environment and the enjoyment of largemouth bass fishing with a fly rod on
warm water lakes, ponds and rivers. More than that,
Jack Ellis brings to these pages the intelligence of a
Phi Beta Kappa graduate from the University of
Southern California.

    Jack Ellis grew up fly fishing the cold-water
rivers and lakes of the Pacific coast. He's cast the long
rod for trout from the Rocky Mountains to Alaska's
Bristol Bay region, and he's even captained salt-water
charter boats. But Jack now plies his skills on his
adopted warm waters of east Texas. My earliest
impression of Jack, through his articles, and later from
his book *The Sunfishes*, was that here is a Renaissance
man speaking for a group of anglers who are little
represented in the available fly-fishing literature. Jack
speaks of bayous and mud puppies, splat fishin' and
hydrilla, and other things Southern. He writes about
"bass fishermen," as opposed to "fly fishermen," and
in this book Jack enters into the murky waters of the
definition of fly fishing.

    One of the appeals of fly fishing is that we

have the freedom, within minimal legal constraints, to decide on our own angling rules—our own pursuit of happiness. For a very few remaining stalwarts, upstream casting of dry flies for trout is the only acceptable form of "true fly fishing." Over a century ago Dr. Henshall "protest(ed) against claiming for it (the dry fly) a higher niche in the ethics of sport than wet-fly fishing." Most modern fly fishers have added wet flys, nymphs, streamers and various nondescript attractor flies to the repertoire they are willing to use to deceive fish. Some fly rodders fish exclusively on the surface, others use sinking lines; some fish for only trout, others only salmon, yet others only in the salt.

Warm-water fly fishers have long accepted cork-body popping bugs as acceptable lures for bass and panfish. They've been quick to utilize plastic foam, mylar tinsel, crystal flash, rubber legs, plastic eyes, silicone, larva lace, super glue, epoxy, and a shoebox of other synthetic materials. Jack Ellis suggests that the fly fisherman consider another step in the evolution of *Bassin' with a Fly Rod*. It's not a difficult step to take, no more so than the transition from bamboo to fiberglass to graphite fly rods. Jack has established his own definition of fly fishing, different from some readers, but it works for him, and he's willing to share everything he's learned. I'm absolutely certain he catches a lot more bass than most other fly rodders.

Somewhere around the early 1970s the fly fishing industry predicted a tremendous growth in fly fishing for bass. Tackle and equipment had improved, interest in fly fishing was growing, new flies were developed. But the anticipated growth never occurred. Jack concludes, and my personal experience confirms, that deep-water bass continue to be too difficult to catch using conventional fly rod techniques. It is too much work and not enough fun. Jack proposes some solutions. These are ideas born of actual fishing experiences based on Jack's constant observations, experimentation and flexibility. These are ideas worthy of consideration by all warm water fly fishermen. These are ideas that will help you catch more bass. The closeminded need not apply.

DICK STEWART

# ACKNOWLEDGMENTS

With gratitude:

To my old friend, Jeff Hines, for his usual moral support and the loan of desperately needed old books.

To that librarian's librarian, Flora Wilhite, who is no stranger to fly fishing herself, and her fine staff at the Sterling Library in Baytown, Texas, for locating many references from the dim past of warmwater angling.

To Dick Stewart, whose help, encouragement and support made this project possible.

To our "guru," Brooks Bouldin, for giving me access to his personal library even though I was writing a book with which he would not agree.

To Joe Messinger, Jr. for bringing his father back to life for me.

To Tom Nixon for his needed approval of this project.

To Don Davis of the Diamondback Corp. for explaining why I like my fly rod.

To Lester Lehman for sharing his extraordinary fly-tying skills.

To Art Scheck and Joe Migliore of Abenaki Publishing for helping to steer me in the right direction, even though I didn't want to listen. Parts of this work have appeared in past articles in *American Angler*, and in my column, <u>Reflections on the Pond</u>.

To Scientific Anglers sales representative, John Mazurkiewicz, for the information on fly lines.

To Burl, Junior, James, Billy and David Judalet, Billy Cards and all my other bass fishing friends who taught me about old Mr. Bigmouth.

To my neighbor, John Jordan, and the good folks of Tyler County, Texas who tolerate my constant trespassing on their ponds and lakes.

And last, but certainly not least, to my devoted wife, Darlene, who puts-up with my fishing addiction and makes a living for both of us.

Thanks, y'all

# INTRODUCTION

Most of us remember grandpa's old fly rod. This curious, long, wispy stick of bamboo with funny little guides and its reel seat in the wrong place usually leaned in the corner gathering dust. Every now and then, grandpa would pick it up and a little smile would cross his lips as his mind drifted back to a simpler time; back to a long-forgotten creek, lined with virgin hardwood; back to a catapulting native bass with a yellow Peck's popper in its mouth.

Compared to our high-speed bass boats, precision tackle and electronic gadgetry, grandpa's fly rod was crude, inefficient and unsophisticated. It was hard to cast, hard to play a fish and the slightest mistake would wrap the whole thing around your neck. Learning to handle one of those outfits was a frustrating, time-consuming challenge, requiring months, even years, of patience and practice. Today, a nine-year old can learn to cast a modern spinning outfit in five minutes. But, grandpa's old fly rod had one thing going for it—it was a whole lot of fun! And this, after all, is what sportfishing is all about.

Many of us are discovering that, in our mad dash of twentieth-century progress, we have left behind many precious aspects of the past. There was a certain aesthetic quality to grandpa's fly fishing. The graceful arc of the line seemed to defy gravity as it swept back and forth in curving loops, the cast ending with the popper landing lightly next to the cypress roots. His pulse raced as the wild fish broke the stillness of the foggy morning with a dissonant splash and a spectacular leap. The bronze warrior darted frantically around the little pool but grandpa finally eased him up on the muddy bank, with the long rod bent nearly double. It is a scene that's seldom repeated in this age of stiff graphite rods, level wind reels and megabucks tournaments.

The creeks of grandpa's youth ran cool and clear under a canopy of ancient hardwood. They were accessible too; underbrush was scarce in the perpetual shade of the primeval forest and posted signs were rare. Deep holes hosted lots of bass and several kinds of bream. The rich, muddy bottom was teeming with all sorts of aquatic insects, crustaceans and amphibians, which provided a limitless smorgasbord of protein for gamefish and catfish alike. Older Southerners remember many happy summer days, trudging barefoot along the creek (fire ants were still in South America) with a cane pole or, if they could afford one, a fly rod.

The virgin timber has been replaced with pine plantations, the fertile creek bottom is smothered with sandy siltation and the banks are lined with impenetrable thickets. Millions of federal dollars came from our New Deal benefactors for massive hydroelectric projects and flood control. The dam building continues today and huge impoundments dominate every southern river. Powerful boats became affordable and revolutionary advances in fishing tackle relegated grandpa's old fly rod to the shed—a relic of the past, valued only as a nostalgic reminder of days long gone.

Throughout the country fly fishermen are rediscovering the simple pleasures of old-style fishing. Many of our creeks may be spoiled, but we still have hundreds of ponds and stock tanks that are teeming with bass; the old river lakes are still hidden in the woods along the Neches and the Calcasieu, the Suwanee and the Pearl. The big "fish flies" still hatch every June. The sight of an old timer "splat fishin'" with a vintage fly rod and wooden popping bug is now only a memory on the bayous, but a new generation of fly fishers is beginning to take his place. The long rod is not, to be sure, the most effective way to catch warmwater fishes but modern anglers no longer equate angling success with a full ice chest. Most serious bass fishermen now recognize the virtues of catch and release, while lower bag limits encourage the practice. Although the competition-oriented sportsman would certainly not want to handicap himself with a fly rod, other anglers, all across the American heartland, seek quieter pleasures—the solitude of a few hours in the woods; the profound spiritual and intellectual rewards of melding with nature; the nourishing and healing the soul.

The fly fishing experience is not for everyone. It does little to satisfy man's primal instinct to pursue and kill wild creatures nor is it an effective way to prove one's masculinity—those so motivated will find few rewards in the gentle, artistic pastime of fly fishing. But the meditative student of nature will discover infinite delights in the quiet elegance of this ancient outdoor sport. The afficionado of the long rod soon finds that fly fishing is more than an avocation; it becomes a philosophy of nature, even a way of life, and complements one's spiritual quest for inner peace. The fly fisher does not have an adversarial relationship with nature. Instead, he or she seeks to enjoy the shrinking natural world without negatively impacting its fragile beauty.

Most fly fishers claim that the ambience is everything and the size or number of fish they catch is quite irrelevant; that the actual fishing is merely a vehicle, an excuse perhaps, for such enjoyment of nature. While no real fly fisher measures the success of an outing by pounds or inches, everyone who approaches the water with a rod likes to catch fish and even the most idealistic of anglers will be a little disappointed when he fails to do so. I still have a good time when I go fishless, but I have a better time when I catch a few. This book presents the argument that we may have gone too far in our quest for aesthetic excellence; that our sport is losing all connection with its practical origins and is in danger of sterilizing itself into historical oblivion. Past generations of anglers, fly fishing legends like Ray Bergman and Joe Brooks, acknowledged the behavioral differences between trout and bass. They recognized that while the tactics of the trout stream may be applicable to farm pond bluegills, they did not belong on a bass lake; a distinction that we seem to have lost in recent years.

This is a practical fishing book about catching fish—wild, elusive fish—that survive and flourish in crowded public lakes, close-to-home waters that are within hours of virtually every fly fisher in the country. It's also about rediscovering old strategies and accepting new challenges; about overcoming prejudices and counterproductive mind sets; about refusing to be intimidated by big waters, powerful boats and hardware slingers. It's about fishing for largemouth bass in quiet waters south of the Mason-Dixon line. But most of all, this book is about Mr. Bigmouth himself, that down-and-dirty street fighter who is probably the most popular gamefish in America.

# ONE

# REAL FLY FISHING

*"It is possible that in the future we will finally come around to fishing for our bass species in something of the manner of dry fly fishing for trout."*

Robert Page Lincoln, 1952

I was almost afraid to shut-off the outboard motor. If it failed to start again, I would probably have to spend the night with the mosquitoes and prowling 'gators in a remote, seldom-fished area of a muddy, unpopular lake. A half mile of ugly mud flats and an hour of arduous poling lay ahead. I hoped that I would be able to get back out; that the wind wouldn't force me deeper into the swamp; that the lake level wouldn't suddenly drop. Inches were critical. I sweated, groaned and struggled through the mud, increasingly convinced that I had made a horrible mistake. At least there were pine trees on the distant bank and that meant dry land, so I could always hike to the high-way—unless the shoreside foliage was impenetrable.

I felt like Dorothy awakening in Oz as the boat abruptly slid into clear, deeper water and my sepia-tone world was replaced by a gorgeous floral display of purple hyacinth, yellow water lilies and the tiny white blooms of subsurface hydrilla. An enormous blue heron rose in flight, squawking disapproval at my intrusion. A mother nutria led her three youngsters toward the thick mat of floating hyacinth that extended a hundred feet from a dense thicket of vine-laced wax myrtle and scrub willow. The hyacinth ended in a well-defined border where the hydrilla, its tops several inches below the surface, continued into the deeper creek channel. I had guessed right. It hadn't rained in a week and Rush Creek, a small tributary of the Neches River, formed a narrow line of lovely clear water that extended a mile down the bank. The beauty of the place alone justified the effort.

I was fumbling through my fly box when a resonant splash broke the stillness of this beautiful June day. I looked up in time to see the last of several minnows disappear down the gullet of a greedy little bass. With trembling fingers, I tied a size 10 Fathead Diver to the 2X tippet and attempted to present it to the feeding fish. It fell several feet to the right of the target area. I was preparing to pick up for another try when a foot-long torpedo rocketed toward the fly, its green dorsal pushing a mound of water ahead and throwing a pronounced wake behind. Nerves frozen, I almost failed to strike when the diver was sucked under in a swirl. The real world seemed distant as I admired this handsome, wild fish, inhaled the damp fragrance of the living swamp and listened to countless birds in their festival of song.

As the day progressed I found that blind casting was counterproductive. The bass were under the hyacinth and my fly not only failed to bring them out, it seemed to frighten them. It was more effective to simply sit quietly, wait until a fish showed, and sight cast to the rise. When one of these spirited little bass darted out of the weeds in pursuit of a minnow, I placed the fly in its path and began an immediate panic retrieve. These fish were all small by Texas standards—"hawgs" prefer to root around on the bottom looking for crawfish and salamanders—but I won't soon forget the sight of those water-pushing dorsal fins as the bass charged my fly. It was challenging, rewarding and indescribably thrilling—one of those glorious times that justify our devotion to this sport. The euphoria of the moment made the return trip across the mud flat a lot easier than coming-in.

Fly fishing for bass is synonymous with topwater action; casting floating or shallow-running flies to feeding, or at least active, fish. It's this "dry-fly" aspect of the fishery, the savage, explosive take of an aggressive largemouth, that I have fallen in love with. I have done my share of both trout and saltwater fishing, but there's just nothing to equal that heart-stopping eruption of water when one of these fellows, even a small one, grabs my bug. I experience this countless times a year and every single fish is just as exciting as my first Texas bass fifteen years ago. I never get tired of it.

### IMITATING TOPWATER FOOD FORMS

Every bass lure will fit, although sometimes roughly, into one of two general classes: those that address the fish's feeding urges, like a plastic worm or a Dahlberg Diver, and those that are designed primarily to trigger the bass's territorial instincts, like a spinner bait or a big, yellow, cupped face popper. Some topwater bass flies, like Jim Stewart's Spin-N-Jim and Buzz Bug, are clearly creations that anger the bass, while others, like Dave Whitlock's Mouserat or Tom Farmer's wonderful little frog quietly seek to imitate actual organisms. The latter logically divide into three additional categories—divers, sliders and, depending upon how they are tied and fished, bugs. Each represents certain food forms and the angler will draw more strikes by trying to imitate a specific organism when manipulating the fly. Consistent success requires observing the behavior of natural organisms and the bass's reaction to them. It also pays to note the type of habitat where each food type is found and keep that knowledge in mind while fishing.

Bugs (or "chuggers" as we say in Texas) are by far the most widely used bass flies and the easiest to fish. I would guess that the vast majority of fly-rod largemouth are taken on bugs. Whether constructed of deer hair, cork, wood, foam or hard plastic, all chuggers float and make varying degrees of commotion when retrieved. The bug will serve as either an attractor or a food form, depending on the type of action the angler imparts to it. True sliders ride low in the surface film and, like the swimming reptiles they represent, make little or no disturbance. For the purposes of this discussion, the term "bugs" includes poppers, many flies that are misnamed "sliders," and any other bass flies that fish on top of the water and make a commotion.

Contrary to conventional wisdom, the popular flat-face hair bug does not seem to effectively represent a small frog. Frogs don't "chug" and they don't float on top of the water. They dive and swim, but I never see them "gurgling" along on the surface.

When the frog fly is fished that way, it may be appealing to the bass's territorial instincts but I do not believe it is stimulating a feeding urge. Frogs usually remain submerged and absolutely motionless and that's when the bass is most likely to grab them. For these reasons, a sparsely-tied Dahlberg seems more appropriate around reeds and other "froggy" habitat than any noisy bug or popper.

*Poppers and bugs are designed to struggle in the surface film.*

## BUGS

A large part of the pleasure derived from fly fishing stems from our awareness of the ecosystem, our observations of nature and the presentation of food forms that represent organisms that live in the waters we fish. Despite the fact that bass are very opportunistic and will attack most any believable offering without hesitation, at least when the fish are surface-oriented, I prefer to offer an imitation that is appropriate. It's not that the diver fishes better in froggy habitat (although it does), it's more a matter of personal satisfaction and aesthetic gratification. Tom Farmer (see his wool-bodied frog in *Flies for Bass & Panfish*, p.13) is an example of a warmwater fly tier who, in the finest traditions of the sport, is guided by his observations of the natural world.

In fact, a standard bass bug doesn't effectively imitate any aquatic or amphibious organism; rather, I think it represents something that has fallen in the water. The bass likely mistakes the bug for a large terrestrial insect, or an injured bird, or even a hapless mammal of some kind. My bug is not at home in the water; it is trapped in an alien environment, struggling, drowning, dying. It is a newborn squirrel or fledgling woodthrush that has tumbled from its treetop nest, or a spent cicada that, having deposited its eggs in the branches of an ancient oak, has fallen into the pond to die. It could be one of those giant carrion beetles that I saw sharing a 'possom carcass with several turkey vultures yesterday, or maybe a fat spider, its abdomen distended with eggs, knocked from the web by cavorting raccoons. State-of-mind is crucial to angling success and, regardless of which fantasy creature I conjure, my bug draws more strikes if I think in such terms and concentrate on imitating the imaginary organism. This multiplicity of food forms is why I find temperate southern climes more fascinating than the frigid waters of the western mountains.

I use the bug in places where such landborne critters might fall to the water—under tree limbs, near big brush piles or where the feeder creek enters the pond. Large, trapped terrestrials are less likely over submerged weedbeds, or in other open water areas, so I prefer a diving minnow or frog in those habitats. My rabbit-strip slider works everywhere—after all, the water snake and its deadly cousin, the cottonmouth, roam the whole pond—but it's most effective during active feeding periods. When Mr. Bigmouth is "off-the-bite," which is most of the time, you need a large, noisy offering that will trigger his natural opportunism. The slider doesn't create sufficient commotion to bring him to the surface.

With the exception of an adult mammal, most terrestrial organisms are helpless in the water. The warmwater tyro invariably retrieves the bug in foot-long strips, a normally unproductive technique. It is far better to achieve the desired chugging action with as little lateral movement as possible, since the animal is struggling, not swimming. When the bug lands, slowly remove all slack from the leader and line but do not move the lure itself until all the rings have disappeared. The bass will slide back into cover when the fly hits the water and then, after a period of time, it will cautiously ease toward the fly. Relax and wait awhile. Then, using the Whitlock straight-line technique, give the bug a solid, deliberate "pop." With practice, you can make the bug chug without moving it more than a couple of inches. Let it sit a few moments between subsequent pops.

*A slider represents an unsuspeccting organism leisurely going about its business.*

The actual food forms present in southern waters do not seem to warrant the garish colors and gaudy designs that have traditionally characterized bass flies. Too many warmwater tiers engage in wild flights of fancy at the vise with little conception of the organisms they are attempting to imitate. Since I began to collect and observe the natural food forms, I now have an actual animal in mind when I tie. To be sure, bass are territorial and will attack all sorts of bizarre lures and attractor flies, but I derive deeper rewards from my angling by trying to appeal instead to the fish's feeding urges. I tie all of my bass flies in drab shades of olive, brown, black and gray.

## FISH SLOWLY

*"Never be in a hurry when fishing a bass bug. The slower you can do it, the better the results."*

*John Alden Knight, 1949*

Discipline yourself to slow down and never start popping the bug right away unless you have some specific reason to do so. It seems that every time I turn to chat with a companion or watch the wildlife, my bug disappears in an explosive boil. That ought to tell me something!

A fast retrieve may sometimes be necessary to discourage pesky bluegills, and certain flies that represent swimming animals, such as Bill Lambing's deadly Hairy Mouse Slider or Whitlock's Mouserat, work best with a "panic" retrieve. Bass may also respond to a rapidly-moving fly when they are aggressively feeding, especially in a schooling situation, or in the presence of current. No fishing rule is absolute. A friend called last spring to chastise me for telling

him to fish slowly. It seems that he was fishing with
Dr. Ed Rizzolo, a superb angler who is as much at
home on a Texas reservoir as a Scottish salmon river,
and Ed was taking fish after fish with a rapidly-
retrieved Dahlberg Diver while his companion had
little action with the same fly and a slow retrieve. Ed
told me later that the bass were feeding heavily under
optimum conditions. Experienced anglers, like Ed,
sense when special circumstances call for a more rapid
retrieve; but stillwater largemouth, especially the
bigger fish, are normally reluctant to chase down a
fleeing organism.

Except for occasional brief flurries like the
above, bass hunt by ambush in pond habitat. A small
fish is most likely to get ambushed when it is preoccupied with feeding, so it is common to see a large
bass cruising among juvenile sunfish that seem
completely oblivious to its presence. The sunfish
keep their eyes on the bass, but they are not worried
because they know that the bass won't pursue them
under those conditions—it doesn't have enough
speed and it takes too much energy. The bass must
catch the sunfish completely by surprise—normally
when they are feeding on an insect hatch or leisurely
cruising the bottom for tidbits of food. So it makes
sense to move the diver or streamer very slowly to
imitate a feeding sunfish. A Diving Minnow that's
retrieved with long, steady pulls is usually less effective than one that makes several short darts and then
remains motionless for ten seconds or so—but there
are exceptions.

I can't emphasize the importance of imitating
the behavior of living organisms strongly enough. The
other day, I saw a rather rare occurrence: an adult
dragonfly, a huge green darner, was trapped in the
surface film. I thought the big insect was dead, a
spent female, and was not surprised when it was
ignored by a passing bass. I was amazed, however,
when this beautiful creature, its long, iridescent body
glistening in the morning sun, began heaving itself
forward with great lunges in a futile attempt to regain
the air. Those powerful wings worked like oars,
pulling the entire thorax out of the water, as it applied
all of its strength in an effort to break free from the
surface film. The weary insect then rested for at least

a minute before continuing its exertions. The commotion initially attracted several curious bluegill, but they were intimidated by such a large insect and kept their distance. The darner rested once more, remaining unnoticed until it resumed what can best be described as a "butterfly" swimming stroke, which only then aroused the interest of a sizable bass that had been lurking in a nearby brush pile. The fish watched intently, its pectoral fins fanning in a circular motion and its body quivering with anticipation, while the doomed dragonfly rested for a third time. When the huge insect resumed its struggle, the bass attacked with lightning speed and merciful finality.

There is a valuable lesson here. At least two minutes elapsed between my first observation of the resting insect and its final demise. During most of that period the dragonfly lay resting on the water and, even while struggling, it made little lateral headway. Consider the implications of this and you will appreciate why we must discipline ourselves to move at nature's speed. The warmwater angler should strive to effectively imitate the behavior of natural food forms. This requires a lot more skill, patience and experience than simply letting the current carry the offering to a waiting taker as happens in rivers and streams.

You are most likely to spook a fish when presenting a cast. When the bug lands near its lair, the bass will ease back into the cover. If the bug remains still for awhile—maybe as much as a minute—the bass will ease out a bit and stare intently at it. When it pops once, the fish may move closer and freeze again. The next time the bug moves the bass will likely attack at lightning speed. This takes time and cannot be accomplished in a twenty second presentation. A minute can be an eternity when you're eager to start gurgling the bug, and some of us have to actually count out loud to keep the fly in the water that long. I watched and counted as a novice fly fisher, a gentleman that I have been instructing for the past year, fished a pond. Each of his casts was actually on the water for an average of seven seconds! Ray Bergman got pretty blunt about this in addressing his fishing companion some sixty years ago: "Every time your plug hits the water the fish beat it. By the time they get over their scare, your plug is back in the boat. Try leaving it alone for awhile!" I similarly chastised my student.

Another common error is failing to fish out a misplaced cast (missing the target and immediately picking up the fly to try again). I know one guy who thinks every cast has to be perfect. He curses and false casts, his oaths reaching ever-deepening levels of depravity, until he finally hits the target. By this time, of course, he's disturbed the water and the terrified bass are cowering somewhere in the depths. It makes sense to fish out every cast, even if it's way off the mark.

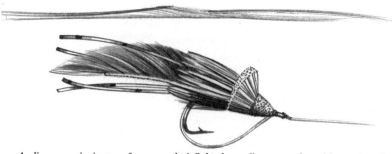

A *diver can imitate a frog or a baitfish*, depending upon how it's retrieved.

### SMALL BASS ON LIGHT TACKLE

The overwhelming majority of the bass that I catch on topwater flies are under 16 inches long and I don't need 9-weight gear to handle them. Every farm pond has a couple of fat old lunkers lurking in the depths and one will occasionally grab my fly, but it's not a daily occurrence. Even in public lakes that are famous for big bass, I still catch mostly twelve to sixteen inch fish—because I am targeting those and not using the baits and techniques required to take trophy fish. Smaller largemouth are more likely to be surface-oriented, to frequent the shallows and to school on baitfish. They are very abundant (especially with the fourteen-inch minimum size that many states have adopted), easier to find and more willing to bite. They are a lot more interesting to the fly fisher than those fat old "hawgs" that spend most of the time lethargically rooting around on the bottom. Those pot-belly types don't even fight well. I accidentally took an eleven pound sow from a farm pond last year.

I happened to have a heavy tippet on my size 2 bug and there was no brush or other obstruction in the immediate area. I thought I had hooked one of the big channel catfish that live in that pond until I actually saw the fish. It was a very disappointing, deep, sluggish fight. I didn't even take a picture—the fish was too grotesque! Younger bass are streamlined and handsome, but, like the rest of us, they lose their looks when they get old and fat.

The habitat you'll be fishing should be the main determinant in fly tackle selection. My favorite rig is a 3-weight rod and a size 8 hair bug or diver, but I obviously can't use that set up in heavily-cluttered waters, even if fishing for the smallest bass. I can't drag fish through weeds, over logs, or skid them across the lily pads with light tackle, of course, but I can fish the edges of cover. With a 2X tippet, I still have enough muscle to steer all but the largest fish into adjacent open water. Whenever I have logs, brush or vegetation between me and the target zone I have to use heavier gear: 6, 8 or 10-weight outfits depending on both the type of fly and the size of the fish I expect to catch. Although I have learned what kind of bass to expect from the various ponds and lakes that I fish, I do get surprised now and then and lose a lunker. I always crimp my barbs and use a short tippet so only a small amount of leader is left hanging out of the fish's mouth. I want any victorious bass to eject the fly and any trailing leader quickly. It's unusual for a big bass to grab a small fly. Large warm-water fish normally won't rise to a minuscule offering.

It's light tackle heaven when largemouth school on baitfish during the summer! Comparatively small bass in open water permit me to use my 3-weight outfit all day without a worry.

## SCHOOLING BASS

Some of the best southern fishing of the year takes place from July through September. Black bass venture into open water to take advantage of the summer bounty of threadfin shad and other schooling baitfishes. When pods of boiling, feeding fish suddenly materialize on a huge southern impoundment, I often forget that I'm on fresh water. The scene is reminiscent of a school of bluefish in Chesapeake Bay or Pacific bonito in the Catalina Channel. When bass desert their weedy, cluttered home for open water, they also abandon their moody disposition and assume the reckless gullibility of some saltwater species.

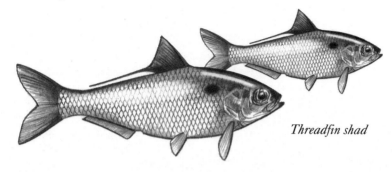

*Threadfin shad*

Although individual, minnow-chasing fish are a common sight in farm pond shallows, genuine schooling activity is restricted to larger lakes with populations of open-water baitfish like gizzard shad, emerald shiners and, especially, threadfin shad. Threadfin cannot survive the cold winter temperatures of small, shallow ponds, but thrive in big reservoirs from Tennessee to the Gulf and west to California. They stay in deep water during the winter, where they are decimated by the voracious white, yellow and striped bass that have been stocked in many of these lakes. Later, they rise to the warm surface in great schools to feed on plankton and other organic matter. In this situation, largemouth bass provide the fly fisher with some great action.

Locating schooling bass is largely a matter of luck, but a few guiding principles do apply. This activity occurs only in summer and early fall on the main lake, but (below the dam) tailwater bass may school on shad that have been sucked through the big generators as late as Thanksgiving Day. Schools form only in the early morning and late evening, normally within a few hundred feet of some sort of structure. Whenever I hear reports of black bass schooling in the deep, open expanses of the lake, further inquiry invariably reveals that they were in the vicinity of a high spot or other submerged structure. I don't head for the lake with the intent of fishing for schooling bass—it's a bonus, not a regular occurrence. After the Fourth of July, I keep my eyes open while fishing and, especially, while running in the boat. Schooling fish may appear any place at any time. Typically, I observe schooling activity in nearby open water while fishing customary habitat with heavier tackle. Bass that reside in heavy cover will move into adjacent open water en masse and gang up on passing schools of baitfish. In late summer and fall, I stay alert for this and periodically look over my shoulder between casts. When "schoolies" show, time is of the essence because they may disappear at any moment! I either start the gasoline motor or use the oars, depending on the distance, pick up the 3-weight that is already rigged with a Marabou Muddler, and head for the school.

I don't get closer than about fifty feet from the bass, so I kill the motor far short of them and coast toward the feeding fish. When I present the streamer to the edge of the activity, the take is instantaneous and almost a certainty. The feeding may be brief or continue for hours. Frequently, schooling fish appear in small groups over a large area, in which case I simply row from school to school. Black bass are intelligent fish and will not tolerate much noise or commotion. Handling the boat with a degree of finesse is imperative for success.

If structure fishing is slow, and the season is right for schooling activity, ride around the lake at half-throttle watching for breaking fish near bottom structure. If you have an electronic depth sounder, make a note of deep schools of shad for later reference. It is also helpful to chat with bass fishermen at the boat ramp—they avoid small-size schoolies, but they will often tell you where you can find them. I have never taken a fish over a couple of pounds in a schooling situation, but the old timers tell me that schools of four and five pounders were once common. Most of the visible fish are in the twelve to fourteen inch range. Uniformity of size seems to be a characteristic of schooling bass, but larger individuals may be hovering beneath the fracas to take advantage of wounded baitfish. I never target the deeper fish because the schoolies are too much fun. The other day, a bass fisherman told me that he had run into a school of little "spots" (spotted bass, the southern version of smallmouth). He said a fly fisher would probably enjoy that. Enjoy it? I'd trade body parts to get into schooling spots!

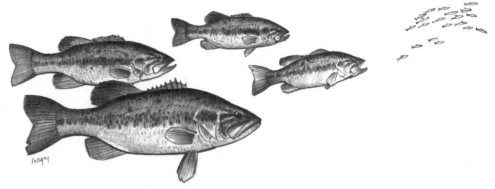

*Always keep in mind the possibility of an encounter with schooling bass.*

One of my regular fly fishing companions, Dr. Guy Harrison, and I recently ran into a school right in the launching ramp cove and took about 25 fish in an hour. This was especially gratifying to me because I had related a scarcely believable incident in a magazine article, about catching lots of fish right at the launching ramp. So I was vindicated that morning. We were amazed that passing boats didn't ruin our fishing. The fish were working right in the narrow channel and another boat would pass through every few minutes using gasoline motors. The fish resumed feeding within a minute or two after each boat passed. I believe, from past experience, if these boats had been operating on their electric trolling motors the bass would have left the area. Gamefish in public lakes get used to people and soon learn that turning propellers, rock-throwing youngsters, swimmers and water skiers are not threatening. The same fish may panic, however, when they hear a trolling motor or a whirling spinner blade because those sounds signify danger. Doug Hannon addresses this behavior in his excellent video, *Understanding Big Bass.*

Schooling bass are completely opportunistic and they will take any fly or lure. This is different feeding behavior than found with trout. Bass know that most any kind of creature could also be in the area, or even feeding on the baitfish, and they take advantage of opportunity when it knocks. I prefer to present an imitation of the baitfish itself and use the Marabou Muddler, in several colors, almost exclusively for schooling bass. Fly recipes are included in Chapter Seven.

Actual schooling is unusual in ponds because there are not the baitfish concentrations found in larger waters, but there's a lovely little lake in the Angelina National Forest that's an exception. A natural "oxbow" lake (formed in an old river channel), it's very deep and threadfin shad are able to survive the winter. Bass regularly school there on autumn mornings and I fish for them with my 3-weight outfit from a float tube. I am usually all alone and it's absolutely delightful. Unfortunately, a power boat is required to chase schoolies on bigger lakes. There's too much water to cover and you can't keep up with the fish unless you have a motor.

Any event that draws small sunfish and other forage species out of the cover will stimulate the bass's feeding urge. Bass may not respond directly to hatches of aquatic or terrestrial insects, but the activity of baitfish feeding on insects stimulates the bass into visible, aggressive feeding behavior. Rural people often keep domesticated catfish that must be fed daily. The catfish generally stay in the feeding area and, as long as they are well fed, they do not overly interfere with the life processes of wild fishes. The bluegill will, however, mill around among the feeding catfish and clean up any tidbits of food that are left. Bass are often observed maliciously lurking around the periphery with their eyes riveted on the preoccupied sunfish. The farmer is unwittingly creating a "secondary hatch" of baitfish with his pellets that draws bass into the area. Most serious catfish growers detest bass and group them with snakes, skunks and hawks—predatory varmints that should be killed.

## FISHING FROM THE BANK

Except during periods of extreme heat or cold, pond bass spend most of the time hiding in shoreside cover, ready to ambush minnows, young sunfish, large insects, amphibians and juvenile reptiles. The best way to stalk and take such fish, which are often quite visible to the angler who quietly observes the situation, is to sneak along the bank undetected and present the offering with a very short overhead or bow-and-arrow cast. The techniques are precisely the same as used to fish a small, brushy trout stream, but the jolting explosion of a largemouth bass grabbing a size 2/0 fly a few feet from your face can only be described as "mind blowing." The hiding bass may think it's concealed, but, with Polaroid glasses and careful observation, the slight fanning movements of caudal and pectoral fins will reveal the fish. Delicately present a bug right in front of the bass with a bow-and-arrow cast—no fly line, just the leader—and don't move it until he shows an interest. The bass may slip back into the weeds a bit when the fly lands. Then, after a few moments, when it begins to ease toward the strange object, pop the bug and hold on. The bass will attack at lightning speed and burst through the surface, perhaps splashing water in your face. It's indescribably thrilling. (The other night one threw water all over my glasses and I couldn't even see!) I held on tightly, and the fish never got its head. The bass just hung there and thrashed, and when released it was still hotter than a firecracker.

All you need is a narrow slot in the vegetation for the bow-and-arrow cast, but it does take patience and practice to handle the outfit under those conditions. It helps to pull the fly all the way to the tip when you want to retrieve the bug for another presentation. Then slide the rod backwards until you can

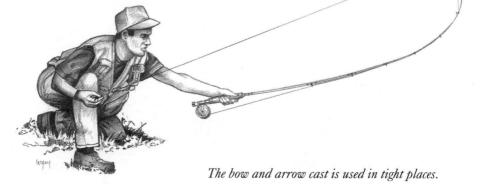

*The bow and arrow cast is used in tight places.*

grasp the fly and pull out enough leader to cast again. If you try to swing the fly back to you it will invariable hang up on weeds or brush. Under more open conditions, short overhead casts may be possible.

In many habitats, spawning bass are really accessible only from the bank. They invariably nest in the heaviest cover available—way back in the brush, behind fallen timber or underneath low branches in mere inches of water. Casting to such places from a float tube is impractical, even unethical, since there is no chance of landing the fish even if you do manage get the fly in there. The location of a nest is betrayed by swirls on the water or the movement of grasses or weeds. It may be an arduous chore to get into casting position, requiring a trek through snake-infested thickets, but don't be in a hurry; plan the whole presentation carefully. The male fish will be visible, hovering over the nest, and a strike is almost a certainty. If the fish passes at the fly without taking it or slaps it with its tail, change patterns and continue presenting the fly until the fish becomes so irritated that it mouths the bug. The male will return to the eggs immediately after release, but if the sow is also present I do not cast to the nest—rather, I give the lovers a bit of privacy and search elsewhere.

The brush and timber that surrounds my home waters may be a fly caster's nightmare, but it allows me to conceal myself. Ranchers often build their stock tanks (basically a watering hole) in open pasture, however, and grazing cattle keep the banks free of weeds and brush. Such ponds receive a lot of nitrogen from both the animals and periodic applications of chemical fertilizer to the surrounding pasture, resulting in extremely fertile habitat and superb fishing. The tanks are necessarily located in low areas and the upward slope of the weedless bank allows the fish to see an angler from some distance. Fish seem to distinguish between a cow and an angler, ignoring the former but avoiding the latter. It's not unusual to see bass feeding around the legs of wading cattle, only to flee in panic when I approach. A low profile is called for here and I sometimes cast to the shallows across twenty or more feet of dry land. All the fly line may be on the ground with only the leader and fly in the water.

If you see wakes moving out of the shallows, stop casting, sit down and patiently wait until the spooked fish regain their composure and resume normal activities. Time spent silently waiting and watching is not wasted because relaxed observation will reveal much to the studious angler. You may detect subtle movements of cattails or other reeds, indicating the presence of spawning or feeding bass, or you may even see the fish themselves as they cruise the bank. Much of our farm pond fishing involves sight casting to visible feeding, spawning, cruising or basking bass.

### BASKING AND CRUISING BASS
On the warmer days of spring and fall, it is common to see bass lying quietly in the shallows, in full view of prey and predators alike. They seem to be sleeping and will ignore your offering, even moving a foot to one side to make room for the passing fly. After spring floods, when lakes are high, I work my boat through the flooded timber and brush until I reach the shallows adjacent to the normally ill-defined bank. I can often see numerous basking bass lazily resting among the grasses and weed stalks. They are not feeding, so you need to understand their territorial nature to induce a strike.

*Basking in the shallows.*

Here's where all those huge attractor flies, spinner baits, buzz baits and other bizarre lures come into the picture. An adult bass has a contentious disposition, a temper if you will, and considers the water around it to be its space. The fish may ignore plastic worms, streamers, divers, hair bugs and any other food form, both real and phony, but will savagely attack something that violates its privacy. Pick the biggest, gaudiest, noisiest thing in your box, preferably something with a spinner blade on it, and cast it right in front of the bass, making the fly as irritating as possible. It must behave like a real creature though—you can't make big splashes, cast the fly line on the fish, or do anything that might panic the fish. Gurgle the fly, pop it in little short jerks, let it sit for awhile and gurgle it some more. If the fish doesn't take, swim it far enough away so the pick up doesn't spook the bass, and present the fly again. If the bass still doesn't respond, change to another big attractor and keep up the pressure. If all that fails, try an unweighted spinner bait—that will be more than the fish can take.

You will also observe non-feeding fish slowly cruising along the bank during mid-day, in full view, often in the company of minnows and little bream. While such fish are more likely to grab an easy meal than are the baskers, they are not in a feeding mode and may be quite difficult to catch. Your best shot here is to simulate an injured baitfish. This will likely require a fly rod version of a casting plug, but a Dahlberg Diver, tied sparsely so it can dive deeply, often brings a strike. This is an excellent application for those deer-hair "plug flies," tied by the talented Jim Stewart of Florida, or Mike Huffman's deer-hair Sunfish. Neither Mike's fly, nor a similar Jimmy Nix pattern worked for me until Mike, an extraordinary fly tier of the "Dallas school," showed me how to counterbalance the fly. A bit of lead wire on the hook makes it rides vertically and naturally. Another Dallasite, Brian Shivers, ties a deep-body marabou streamer that I have also found effective for cruising bass.

There are a number of "action" flies, such as Bob Popovic's Pop Lips Pumpkinseed, or Jim Stewart's Spin-N-Jim and Buzz Bug that are specifically designed for nonfeeding bass. I warn you, though, that these patterns can be agonizingly diffi-

cult to tie. It's easier, if less rewarding, to just go down
to your tackle dealer and buy a few small plugs. For
the dedicated tier, these flies are all described in *Flies
for Bass & Panfish* by Dick Stewart and Farrow
Allen—our only pattern "bible" and a must on any
warmwater angler's bookshelf.

### NYMPHING FOR BASS

While bass eat primarily fish, along with the occasional crawfish and salamander, they will not turn
down a big Odonata (dragonfly or damselfly) or
*Hexagenia*, nymph. I don't think bass grub around in
the mud searching for them, at least I've never
observed such behavior, but there's no doubt that
they opportunistically eat aquatic insects. I regularly
catch small bass on sinking nymphs while fishing for
bluegills, especially when the fly is moving, and I
miss a lot of bass strikes as well.

*Dragonfly nymph*

The problem with all subsurface fishing for
bass is strike detection. If bass would take an underwater offering as ferociously as they grab a surface fly,
my life would be a lot easier. When a bass picks up a
nymph, it eases up to the fly, opens its mouth, sucks
in the fly (water and all) rolls it around in his mouth
for a few seconds to see if it's real, and then decides
whether or not to swallow the fly. The bass accom-
plishes this procedure without any lateral movement
whatsoever, it doesn't even jiggle a strike indicator. A
bluegill, on the other hand, grabs the nymph, after a
close inspection, and runs with it. Bluegills learn as
juveniles to get away from their peers or have their
meal stolen. A bluegill will quickly eject the phony
nymph too, but it gives a discernible strike first. The
bass does not give a signal, because it did not learn
the same kind of competitive, evasive behavior as
bluegills (and trout). Young bass are less inclined to
school and fight with each other in the wild than
juvenile bluegills. For this reason, subsurface bass
flies must be retrieved. This is true with nymphs,
crawfish, salamanders and many other important bass
foods where a swimming retrieve may be entirely
unnatural and inappropriate. Without the steady
retrieve there is just no way, even with a floating line
and an indicator-equipped leader, to detect the take.
So nymphing for bass is restricted to open waters

where weeds and cover permit such a retrieve, not prime bass habitat.

This is a completely undeveloped field of stillwater fly fishing which presents many confounding problems and challenges, but also fascinating opportunities. I have had some early successes with Harry Murray's Strymph (ibid, p. 69) tied on a size 6 hook, and fished on a long leader with a small slip bobber for an indicator. I have to keep it moving though, and it gathers weeds and frequently snags on underwater brush. Harry's fly is a good imitation of the big darner nymphs that sometimes swim freely, and it is designed to double as either a nymph or a streamer. Unfortunately, my home waters are slightly more cluttered than Harry's river. Tying this fly with an extra fat thorax provides a little weed resistance, but it also impairs hooking efficiency. Weighted flies, however appealing to the bass, are virtually un-fishable in timber but they can be deadly in weed-beds. Nymphing in cluttered, stillwater presents some special challenges, such as tying weed-resistant nymphs. Odonata nymphs are probably an important part of the largemouth's diet, but effective presentation and strike detection will test the mettle of even expert nymph fishermen.

The underwater feeding behavior of the largemouth bass was documented in a fascinating study at Bull Shoals Reservoir. As reported in the October 1982 issue of *Outdoor Life*, a diver spent several hours each day in the company of a group of bass, watching them feed and go about their daily routines. The bass eventually accepted the diver and would eat out of his hand but, and this is hard to believe, they only accepted that particular diver and fled from other similarly attired swimmers. The study confirmed not only the bass's long memory of a particular lure, but also my observations regarding subsurface behavior. When aggressively feeding, bass take a minnow or a surface item with great speed and gusto. Most of the time, however, the bass cruise the bottom looking for nymphs, salamanders, crawfish and the like, which they simply suck-in. In the study, when a slow-moving, bottom-crawling lure was presented to such fish, it was quickly ejected with no lateral movement whatsoever. It is this aspect of bass behavior that frustrates our fly fishing efforts and requires unorthodox solutions.

Fly fishing for lethargic, subsurface large-mouth is theoretically possible, but it demands more perseverance than most of us can muster. It's difficult, horribly frustrating and, to be perfectly honest, not terribly productive. We can effectively address bass with traditional fly fishing methods as long as the fish are visible or at least within a reasonable depth, but more commonly they settle to the bottom or remain motionless while suspended over deep structure. In recent years, a new kind of purism has constrained fly fishers from employing alternative tackle and lures. Past generations of anglers accepted the fact that conventional (real) fly fishing was effective for large-mouth bass only on rare, delightful occasions. They did not hesitate to switch to a casting rod, or to present a strip of pork rind or a metal lure on the fly rod, to non-feeding fish. Those subsurface fly fishing systems that we hear about today—sinking lines with buoyant flies and similar systems—make interesting reading and sell fishing tackle. But such notions are based on an idealistic perception of bass fishing and usually prove to be woefully deficient in actual practice, often frustrating and discouraging would-be bass fly fishers.

# TWO

# WHERE THE BASS ARE

Although largemouth bass may live in any sort of water, from a pristine lake in the Canadian wilderness to a polluted drainage ditch in a Midwestern city, they require massive amounts of forage in order to thrive and grow. Significant numbers of large fish are found in only a few exceptionally rich lakes that sustain healthy populations of shad or other prolific baitfish. Such waters, Lake Fork in Texas for example, are usually new, recently flooded reservoirs that are rich in organic matter to kick-off the food chain. These glamour waters, mostly below the Mason-Dixon line, receive a lot of attention from outdoor writers and tend to be crowded for a few years, until the fishing normalizes. Most fly fishers prefer smaller, uncrowded places, even if they are less accessible or the fishing is not as good.

## FARM PONDS AND SUBDIVISION LAKES

New warmwater fisheries are being created every day by real estate developers all across the American heartland. As the last of the small farmers abandon the land for urban jobs, ponds and tanks that once irrigated crops and watered animals offer inviting homesites for beleaguered city dwellers who are migrating toward the country in increasing numbers. This trend bodes well for the ecological future of rural America. Here in the South, a new wave of homesteaders, largely middle class and well-educated, is changing the face of the land with a refreshingly new commitment to the environment. Developers are motivated not only to minimize the impact on native flora and fauna in planning these subdivisions, but to actually improve the existing ecology of polluted ponds that were once littered with household trash and rusting farm implements. Many of these new and restored fisheries sustain healthy gamefish populations today.

I have lived on private lakes for ten years, as do many warmwater anglers. Each summer morning I celebrate the breaking dawn from my float tube. Bass are usually active in the coolness of morning, and I feel a breathtaking thrill with every pass made at my popping bug, a feeling recalling a Sierra childhood from a half-century past. Many pleasurable experiences become mundane with constant repetition, but the delight of a surface take, regardless of the species, is one of two exceptions to that rule. A wild bass breaking the placid surface of a southern pond to grab a well-tied, well-presented hair bug is no less exciting, no less rewarding than its salmonoid counterpart on a western river. While trout will always have a special place in the heart of every fly fisher, we should recognize that our veneration is based on purely emotional, subjective factors. For years I tried to translate the charm, mystique and tradition of the classical trout stream to a warmwater pond, but the harder I tried the more I pined for the western mountains. I finally grew weary of this counterproductive adherence to tradition and accepted the largemouth bass and its smaller cousins for what they are. That very acceptance has turned waters that I once scorned into a personal angling paradise.

Accessing private water will be, I predict, a major fly fishing issue in the coming decades. Subdivision lakes are only "semi-private" because, in most cases, you only need the permission of one resident to fish the lake. In my area, such subdivisions are so numerous that nearly everyone knows at least one resident. In many rural areas, recreational real estate is comparatively inexpensive and I have acquired lots in several subdivisions just for the fishing access. You would be amazed at just how inexpensive this can be if you don't care about the desirability of the lot as a building site. Before investing in property, however, proceed carefully. Make sure the lake will support fish, that the dam is properly constructed and, most importantly, that the upstream watershed is protected from future development. Also, talk with other property owners to make sure their management ideas are compatible with your own. You wouldn't

want to buy on a lake that's managed strictly for
catfish. One fly fishing acquaintance of mine was
horrified when the other residents of his subdivision
voted to add dye to the lake to make it blue!

Blue-ribbon bass fishing is closely related to
real estate values. It requires the cooperation of all
the property owners, often entails considerable
expense, and will be found in only a few upscale
subdivisions—the kind with 5,000-square-foot homes
on five acre parcels. Inexpensive lots with loose deed
restrictions usually mean more bait fishing and less
catch and release. Bass and other sunfish nearly
always flourish in any subdivision lake, regardless of
the fishing pressure, but they will remain small unless
the larger fish are released and good management
practices are followed. But I don't have a problem
with small, hungry fish; I simply gear down to them.
They are extremely aggressive, fight hard and are
almost always completely wild. The ambience that
pond fishing provides more than compensates for the
fact that the bass are usually smaller than those in
larger bodies of water. There are always a few lunkers
in every warmwater pond, but most of the bass in a
subdivision lake are normally under three pounds.
Small bass behave so differently from the larger fish
that you would think that they are a separate species.
They are more aggressive, feed often, patrol the
shallows, and fall for the same light tackle and flies as
bluegills. With a mid-size, size 6 bug, I can usually
take both bass and bluegills without changing tackle
or strategy. Many of these small lakes can be effectively fished with the same tackle, the same flies, and
basically the same strategy as you would use on your
favorite trout stream or lake. You may be pleasantly
surprised by just how effective your coldwater tactics
are. I appreciate the numerous small bass and just
accept the occasional "big one that got away" rather
than fish all the time with a cumbersome 9-weight fly
rod and a fist-size bug.

Pond bass are rarely well-fed unless their
numbers are low, it is an unusually rich pond, or it is
directly supplied with minnows, crawfish, tilapia or
other natural bass food. It takes a lot of food just to
sustain an adult bass and an incredible amount of
forage—perhaps as much as ten pounds—to add a

pound of body weight. That's a lot of crawfish and minnows, and without a source of nitrogen (a nearby stock yard, sewage treatment plant, septic tanks, grazing stock, fertilized pasture, field crops, or the intentional introduction of nutrients into the pond), population density will probably not exceed a scant ten pounds per acre. That ten pounds can be tied-up in a single leviathan that dominates his acre, but more likely it consists of a dozen skinny runts with big mouths. Even the large fish that we see in such ponds are lean-looking with oversized mouths. A richer pond may support fifty pounds or more of bass per acre, in a healthy population that is made up of differing size fish, but that normally requires very good management. Some waters have been managed by adding supplemental nutrients to the very bottom of the food chain to encourage phytoplankton—adding fertilizer, or depositing hay or other organic matter on the bottom. Bass are often better fed in big reservoirs because large areas of open water are perfect for plankton production, the bass are less concentrated, and the water is deep enough to sustain shad and other prolific baitfish.

Threadfin shad cannot tolerate cold temperatures and require deep water in order to survive the winter, even in Texas. When the water temperature drops to about 60 degrees in the fall, shad become very sluggish and the bass feed on them heavily (if the stripers that have been foolishly introduced will allow them to feed on the shad).

The shores of subdivision lakes are often studded with piers, boathouses, sun decks and similar structures that not only provide shade but can also be a source of food for the juvenile sunfish that make up the bulk of the bass's diet. Residents often throw a daily ration of floating pellets from their pier and enjoy watching the feeding fish. Discriminating anglers abhor this practice because it domesticates the fish. The wild credentials of bluegills that live under the pier are indeed tarnished by artificial feeding, but bass seem more interested in the little bluegills that are preoccupied with eating and are quite vulnerable. Fortunately, the sunfish are remarkably adaptable, thriving in close proximity to man. A large subdivision in my county, with 150 acres of poorly-managed water and 2,000 water-skiing residents,

still produces a number of double digit bass every year. Despite heavy bait-fishing pressure, the bluegill forage holds up quite well.

Night fishing can also be very productive on these lakes, although frustrating and difficult. Don't try it unless you are intimately familiar with the lake. Many of the piers are lighted and attract flying insects, which attract baitfish, which attract bass. The best time to break-out the 9-weight and the big bugs, if that's your bag, is in the wee hours of the morning on a dark, moonless night. Subsurface offerings, especially those that represent water dogs, newts, sirens and other salamanders, will be more effective under a full moon. These amphibians all feed nocturnally.

The upper end of this type of lake is typically shallow, weed choked and hard to fish. The developer often leaves the land surrounding the inlet creek in a natural state as a sort of "commons." Such areas are often wadeable and offer superb fly fishing. The entire population of breeding bass, as well as the smaller sunfish, will probably spawn in this shallow end. If the lake is built on an active spring with a good year-round flow, don't neglect the creek below the dam. Chances are that no one ever fishes there and it's loaded with small bass. Even if the creek seems too small to hold fish as viewed from the dam, there may be deep holes a short walk downstream. Before going down the creek, however, thoroughly fish the area in front of the spillway. Baitfish gather above the overflow to take advantage of minuscule food forms in the passing current. Even on the slowest days, I can usually scratch a bass or two from the overflow area. If the overflow discharges into an adjacent pond, bass will gather right below the spillway for the same reasons.

The quality of fishing in subdivision lakes seems to follow a kind of cycle. There is generally a small cadre of serious bass fishers who usually release their fish. They are the white hats. Black hats are worn by the bait-fishing bulk of the residents who only go fishing when "they're biting." When word gets out that someone caught a "nice mess," the black hats will hammer the lake day after day, month after month, until they have removed a substantial part of the population. The lake is then "fished out," and the bait fishers go away. The white hats know, however, that a fertile warmwater lake will bounce back quickly—in, perhaps only a year or two. They then enjoy several years of excellent fishing if they keep quiet but, if news of good fishing leaks out, the bait fishers will dust off the cane poles and minnow buckets, bring their grandchildren out from the city, don their black hats and the cycle begins anew. If a black hat asks you if you're having any luck, choose one of the following answers: "not much," "pretty slow," or the standard, "a couple little ones."

Many of these folks seem philosophically opposed to the idea of catch and release. I did manage to talk one homeowners association into adopting a catch-and-release policy, after they were faced with a hefty restocking bill, but they insisted on continuing to allow children to kill their fish! That was particularly painful to me because I find that children readily accept the idea of catch and release, and they are much more likely to express an interest in fly fishing and fly tying than adults. I bought my own ponds several years ago and I live so far out in the woods now that I never see any kids, but I used to enjoy the small group of neighborhood youngsters that once gathered around my vise, or followed me along the creek while I fished, collected insects and scouted the spawning beds on our local pond. We once spent a whole summer studying salamanders and their relationship to the fish. I learned more than the kids!

Sometimes the distinction between teacher and student became blurred. I once allowed a twelve-year-old protege to talk me into an adventure I would live to regret. His glowing reports of six-pound bass and enormous bluegills were just too much to resist. "You can see 'em swimmin' around," he said, "I can't pull 'em in—they're too much for me." He assured me that the owner was never there during the week, that the lake was not visible from the main house and, that since no one had told him *not* to go in there, it must be all right.

My partner in crime arrived at the prearranged location the following day after school. He hid his bicycle in a clump of yaupon and held the barbed wire apart while I slipped through. I knew I should

back out at this point and would most certainly regret
dragging that float tube with me. We made our way
through the dense vegetation to the bank of a rather
ordinary pond, which soon gave-up a couple of rather
ordinary bass.

I was thinking "this is not worth the risk I am
taking," when my accomplice suddenly shouted,
"let's get outta here!" The Artful Dodger fled into
the woods but poor old Feagan was stuck in the float
tube and could only watch the cloud of dust as the
pickup rumbled toward the lake at high speed.
Humiliation, terror and visions of steel bars competed
with more rational thoughts of just what I should say
to the cowboy type who now stood on the bank with
folded arms and an icy expression. Trembling, I got
out of the tube and muttered my name but he refused
my extended hand. His attire and demeanor suggested that he was an employee of some sort. I
fumbled with my fin tethers, buying time to devise a
strategy, and tried to recall the name on the Farm
Bureau sign that I had seen hanging on the fence.
Robert something . . . Yes, that's it, Robert and
Cynthia Bryan. Or was it Bradley? Or Branson?

I prayed that the cowboy wasn't Robert
himself and went for the big lie.

"Bob and Cindy have a fine place here," I
said with a feigned grin, "even nicer than they described."

Cowboy didn't buy it. "Dr. Brandin always
calls when someone's comin'. What's that name
again?"

This conversation couldn't continue; I had to
think fast. I assumed an alarmed expression—not
difficult under the circumstances. "Where's my
grandson?" I exclaimed frantically, turning toward the
woods. His stern countenance softened somewhat.
"He can't have gone far," I continued, "excuse me a
moment while I find him." The cowboy nodded,
threw my tube in the back of his pickup and I
quickly disappeared into the forest before he could
offer assistance.

The bicycle was gone. The little rat fink
hadn't even waited for me! I ripped my waders on the
barbed wire and sloshed my way down the dirt road to
my own pickup. At least I still had my rod. I hope Dr.

Brandin (whose name has been changed to protect the guilty) is enjoying the float tube.

My next mistake was relating the incident to my wife Darlene. "Cynthia Brandin is an important customer," she shrieked, "she comes into the office all the time." She snarled something about dying from embarrassment if the Brandins discovered my identity. Her eyes rolled heavenward in a plea for divine guidance when I suggested that, since she knew Mrs. Brandin, perhaps she could intercede on my behalf in an effort to retrieve the tube. I see the cowboy's truck in town occasionally, usually at the feed and hardware store, and assiduously avoid him.

My fledgling fly fishers and I gathered by our home pond the next afternoon to discuss the lesson we had learned from the aborted outing. "Never take a float tube when you sneak-in," admonished the Artful Dodger. One especially bright young lady suggested that, instead of claiming to know the landowner, I should have dropped the name of his neighbor and simply pretended to be in the wrong place. (I pity her future husband.) Little sister was expelled from the class, however, when she lisped that the Artful Dodger should not have taken Mr. Ellis on such a risky adventure because "he's too old to run fast." As a responsible adult, I was obligated to help these children stay out of trouble, so I taught them how to use the bow and arrow cast so they could remain concealed in the brush while fishing—all except little sister. I hope she trips on a vine and gets caught!

## KEEPING IT WILD

Nearly all of our choice ponds are now behind barbed wire on properties like Dr. Brandin's estate. Quality angling is becoming increasingly expensive, whether you choose to spend your fishing budget on Alaskan lodges or, as I have done, on buying your own home water. The fact is that American fly fishing is racing toward private water at breakneck speed. The magazines are full of articles extolling the virtues of private trout ponds in the West and ads for membership trout fishing on Colorado ranches. It's no use to fight this. It's inevitable. It seems to me we should focus our energies and resources on making the best of it.

If properly managed, warmwater lakes can be kept in a relatively wild state as long as indigenous species are stocked and supplemental nutrients are provided only at the lowest levels of the food chain. I don't like to see the introduction of any exotics, not even African tilapia for bass forage or Asian carp for weed control. A pond should be populated only by fishes that were native to the original creek or, at the very least, could have lived in the creek before the dam was built. Some Texas pond owners now purchase a load of rainbow trout every fall for winter sport. The surviving trout serve as bass forage in the spring. The rainbows don't hurt anything, but this is an offensive practice that insults both the trout and the bass. It's on a par with planting smallmouth in a steelhead river, or those cursed stripers in a fertile bass lake. At least we are moving away from the days when natural bass lakes were often poisoned to make room for the hatchery trout!

Our Texas Department of Parks and Wildlife has an unfortunate, but very popular, winter trout-stocking program. They dump thousands of these exotics into Boykin Springs, a small lake near my home, every December. I have it on second-hand, but very reliable, authority that monster double-digit bass wait for the hatchery truck and go on a feeding frenzy when the trout are dumped. One of these days I'm going to visit that pond at night with my 10-weight and a big Lefty's Deceiver streamer fly.

Unlike a high dam on a major river, the construction of a small earthen dam across a creek does not compromise the ecosystem so greatly,

because the pond is normally not deep enough to
significantly affect the temperature of the overflow.
Because nearly all sunfish (with the possible exception of the northern smallmouth) do better in
stillwater, it actually enhances the existing habitat.
Some overflows are constructed in such a way that
water is drained off the bottom of the pond where
oxygen levels are low. This is good for the pond but
could theoretically have a negative effect on life in
the creek for a short distance downstream. If the
overflow comes off the warm surface, as most do, the
dam seems to do no harm unless it is poorly constructed and washes out. A wash out silts the bottom
of the creek and can have terrible effects downstream.
I once saw a whole string of dams fall like so many
dominoes during a tropical storm with disastrous,
long-term consequences for the fisheries. Landown-
ers planning to build a dam should be sure it is done
properly because they may be held accountable for
damage to downstream properties. Also, it is unethical
and, perhaps, illegal to shut the creek entirely off
while the lake is filling. Always let enough water
through to sustain the downstream ecosystem during
that period.

Truly wild, natural warmwater fisheries
disappeared a long time ago, and now the only remaining, really pristine, unmanaged coldwater trout
streams are in Alaska, but they are threatened. For
the time being, the fish in our subdivision lakes are
mostly wild, at least in the sense that the bulk of their
diet consists of natural food forms. While I often
dream of what it would have been like to have fished
these creeks in their original state—clear and clean,
everything in perfect balance, an abundance of
aquatic insects, lots of wild fish—I am grateful nonetheless that I have access to quality fishing a short
walk from my front door.

## FISHING IN A FLOWER GARDEN
Normally I wouldn't be caught dead within ten miles
of a public bass lake on the Fourth of July, but fishing
had been so good all week that I decided to go
anyway. The campground at the state park was
overflowing. A line of trailered boats led all the way to
the highway, at least a half mile, and it was still dark! I

turned down an abandoned farm-to-market road that
now just disappears into the man-made lake. Despite
the early hour, a young couple was preparing to
launch an inboard ski boat on the old roadbed. I told
them the water was too shallow for such a craft like
theirs with a big V-8 engine, but they just stared at
me, my angling attire suggesting ulterior motives.

I inflated my Kikk Boat, grabbed my 8-weight
rod, donned my bulging vest and paddled the familiar
route in the dark. By first light I was deep in a dense
bed of American lotus. I pulled the giant pads aside
with the paddle, hoping Mr. Gator had finished
hunting for the night, and arduously worked my way
toward the small pocket of open
water that I had fished the
previous morning.

The lake was much warmer than the air and a
dense layer of radiation fog hovered over the water,
almost concealing my Grinnel fly as it slithered
through the pads. I saw the wake coming first and
then the open maw as the bass crashed down on the
fly. I gave him no quarter—I couldn't in that cover—
and hoped the twelve pound tippet would hold. It
did, and the fish made the twenty-inch mark, weigh-
ing in at a good four pounds! As he darted back to his
watery bower, I could faintly hear boat traffic out on
the lake but it was too far away to bother me. I was
insulated from all that, hidden in my flower garden—

only the racing engine on the ski boat, as its young
owner tried to extricate the craft from the clinging
mud, disturbed the tranquil morning. As I landed my
fourth fish, I decided that was a small enough inconvenience on a holiday weekend. I later assisted the
young people in getting the expensive boat back on
its trailer and directed them to the nearest suitable
launching site.

Although comfortable mid-summer fishing is
restricted to a few hours early in the morning, and
during rainy or overcast periods, bass may be active all
day in the shade of lily pads or other vegetation.
Largemouth prefer water less than eight feet deep
and will only seek the depths when they can't find
comfort, food and security in the shallows. Lily pads
provide all three, offering the angler a classic fly
fishing experience. This habitat charms me in the
same way that a bucolic meadow stream may charm
my counterpart in Vermont. Here, in a watery garden
of spectacular blooms and dancing dragonflies, the
real world is only a distant memory.

By late spring the shallower areas of many
lakes become choked with lily pads, effectively
closing-off vast expanses of excellent habitat to the
bass boats. They can only penetrate these dense areas
of vegetation with great effort, and the few that do
will have difficulty fishing with conventional tackle.
Most topwater plugs, with their exposed hooks, are
not fishable in this kind of cover and even the reliable
plastic worm lets them down. It is very difficult to
land a bottom-hooked bass through a maze of tough,
leathery lily pad stems. Our weightless offerings are
perfect for these conditions, however, and the leverage provided by the longer rod enables us to keep the
fish on top and thwart his efforts to wrap the leader
around a stem. This is one of the few stillwater
situations where the fly fisher definitely has the edge
over the "heave-and-crank" crowd. Anglers in bass
boats will, however, pound the edges of the beds with
every kind of lure and bait all season, and it is necessary to penetrate the field, which may cover several
square miles in some southern reservoirs, in order to
find blue-ribbon fishing.

Although a typical lily pad field may appear
too dense even for fly fishing, there are usually

hidden pockets of open water back in the interior. Looking at the area from the bank, or standing up in a boat, the entire field may appear utterly impenetrable and unfishable. Such is usually not the case, however, and wherever the water is a little deeper, such as an old creek channel, ravine or gully —any sort of a hole—a little fishable water can be found. Accessing the interior of a typical field is an excellent way to get your aerobic exercise. It requires pulling, poling and paddling through the heavy leaves at an agonizingly slow pace. After several hours of struggle and physical exertion, I may have covered only a half mile and failed to find any place to cast the bug. But when I do find the little area of open water that I seek, the excitement of anticipation makes it all worthwhile. I experience the same adrenaline rush that comes with the thrill of discovery that I knew as a child in the West. No white man had ever walked this far up the creek before; I am surely the first to lay eyes on those little trout finning lazily in the quiet pool. Remember that feeling? I am richly blessed to experience it once again.

It may take several days of exploration to find a hole in the pads, but I can usually fish it regularly all season unless the lake level drops enough in late summer to allow the invasion of these fast-growing plants. The hole will be in the same place every year until, with the passage of time, floods and siltation alter the bottom contour and the open water disappears. The spot I fished on the Fourth of July in 1990 is getting smaller every year and soon it may be completely gone. American lotus, the most prevalent species in my area, occupies this particular field. Yonqupin, which is what the locals call this indigenous plant, grows especially thick. The huge leaves, which are perfectly round and two-feet in diameter, actually overlap each other, leaving no fishable water whatsoever between them. The smaller pads of true water lilies (lotus is not a water lily, botanically speaking), grow less densely and there is normally a little open water surrounding each leaf. The fly will alternately slide over the heart-shaped pads of white and yellow water lilies and through these little pockets of water—unless hydrilla decides to occupy that niche, which is too often the case along the Gulf

Coast. If they are able to get to it, bass cannot resist a
snake or frog slithering through the pads in such a
tantalizing manner.

As you work your way through the field, you
are passing over thousands of bass and other fish
because the vegetation is only on the surface. The
water below is relatively open. Each pad is supported
by a single stem, allowing the bass plenty of room to
maneuver, ambush small fish and to search for the
myriad nymphs, crustaceans, amphibians and aquatic
reptiles that thrive in the organic stew on the bottom.
Water depth averages three to four feet in the beds
and never exceeds about five feet. The foliage dies
each fall, sinks and decays, thereby replenishing vital
nutrients and further enriching the ecosystem with
the sun's energy. Bottom samples will bring up a dark,
smelly compost of decaying vegetable matter that is
often teeming with minuscule organisms of all kinds.

Even if the main lake is murky or off color,
the water back in these beds is usually quite clear.
The vegetation serves as a buffer against the turbu-
lence of wakes and wind and seems to filter muddy or
cloudy water.  Dirt settles on the stems which are
often slimy with mud. In shallow ponds, excessive
growth of water lilies can lower dissolved oxygen
below the bass's minimal requirements, due to the
presence of so much decaying organic matter, but on a
large lake intermixing maintains acceptable levels
even in the heat of summer. Some introduced species
of water lilies become invasive and may
dominate a shallow pond at the
expense of other plants
and animals.

*There usually
are small,
fishable areas
in even the
densest
spread of
lily pads.*

## CREEKS AND TAILWATERS

Neither largemouth bass nor the anglers who fish for them like current, and both strive to avoid it. I am somewhat out-of-step with my southern peers, however, because I do enjoy fly fishing in warmwater creeks and tailwaters—too many years in trout country, I guess. Fly fishing is restricted to low-water periods in late summer and fall. The rest of the year, our creeks carry a great deal of water and are far too turbid for anything but bait fishing. Since I almost always target bream with dry flies, most of the bass I catch in creeks are accidental and quite small.

There are exceptions to every rule, though, as I found out in the Magnolia Hole on Theuvinin's Creek in September a few years ago. This lovely southern creek, which for some inexplicable reason the locals call "Toodle'um," rises in the pineywoods about ten miles north of my place and flows through private land all the way to the Neches River some thirty miles to the south. Most of the watershed is owned by large timber companies and leased to hunting clubs, and a membership in one of the clubs is required to gain legal access to the creek, which consists of a series of sandbar riffles of varying lengths, separated by deep pools of varying sizes. I can always count on several beautiful bluegill, along with a rock bass or two, when I reach the prettiest stretch of all, an extraordinarily long, deep hole, the head of which is dominated by an ancient magnolia tree.

In seasons past, I could count only on the rises, because a mean old largemouth that lived there wouldn't let me land the bluegills! This bass grabbed the sunfish as soon as it was hooked and quickly broke the fine tippet. One day I decided to catch this outsize fish. I returned to the pool with 8-weight gear and offered the bass a size 2 Dahlberg Diver on a 10-pound tippet. The big fish grabbed the diver and headed for the fallen hickory tree that blocks the lower end of the run. I tried to hold on but the tippet snapped. The next day I returned with the heaviest rod in my collection—a 10-weight—and cast a giant Deceiver on a short length of twenty-pound tippet. The bass tore for the dead tree again and this time he made it. As far as I know the Deceiver is still hanging in the submerged branches. This had gone far enough—to hell with sportsmanship—this thing was going to die! The next day I used my saltwater rod and reel, hooked a live, six-inch bluegill on a 2/0 bait hook and, with smug confidence, let it swim out into the pool. It wasn't long until the struggling little bream disappeared in a swirl and I got a good look at the wide, green side of this monster. He wasn't going to break 40 pound line, I assured myself, and held on. Moments later I retrieved the bare hook which was as straight as a nail! My only remaining option was dynamite so I gave up. Unfortunately, the monster bass is not there any more and I miss him. I hope he died of old age.

Although crawfish imitations are very difficult to fish effectively in still, cluttered waters, they do work well on southern creeks that have populations of the naturals. When I see concentrations of the mud "chimneys" that crawfish build along the bank, I drift one of Gary Borger's "swimming female" crawfish (see his *Designing Trout Flies* for the pattern) through the tail of a riffle and into the head of a pool. I let it sink into the quiet depths, then retrieve it very slowly, and am often rewarded with a small largemouth, spotted or, less frequently these days, native redeye bass. The food supply in these creeks is limited and bass are rarely over a pound. The behemoth that lived in Toodle'um Creek was a rarity. That fish probably dominated that pool for years, allowing no other bass to enter, until it grew big enough to eat snakes, birds, big bluegills, maybe even adult bull frogs. Even the otters, which are abundant these days, probably gave him a wide berth. Southern folks once killed otters and other varmints on sight but, since we have become more environmentally concerned, the otter population has exploded in my county.

Bass often move upstream and a creek that enters a reservoir can provide good fishing for some distance above its mouth. Bass boats can only penetrate the inlet cove to the end of navigable water. Above that the terrain is likely overgrown and impenetrable, but there may be a lot of fish on up the creek—again, mostly small ones unless you find a spawning area. It's worth the effort to secure your boat to the bank and work your way through the brush on foot, or try to find a circuitous route through adjacent woods, to gain access to the upper stretches of such a feeder stream. Finding fish where no one goes is a very special experience. You feel that you've discovered your own little secret world. I love and cherish each of these places, even the nasty critters that inhabit them.

This fishing is likely going to require the bow-and-arrow techniques discussed in Chapter One, but you may also discover a large open area of wade-able marsh or flats. Dense thickets, water moccasins and nests of vicious hornets require slow, careful going but, depending on the terrain, there is always the possibility of a hidden "mini-lake" around the next bend—maybe a prime bedding ground that you can visit in the spring. The spirit of adventure and exploration that we knew as children can no longer be found on most heavily-fished trout streams, but it's still alive and well in some remote woods. You can, of course, study aerial photographs of these areas but that takes all the fun out of it. A fly-rod spinner bait is indispensable in such tight habitat because you can flip it, chunk it, sling it and work it with the rod tip. You'll see what I mean when you get into one of these places and try to fish.

The tailwaters below large reservoirs are usually alive with gamefish of all kinds, because they are constantly "stocked" with baitfish that come through the generators. Striped bass have unfortunately taken a heavy toll on these fisheries, but small largemouth and spotted bass are often abundant as well. Since stripers feed on the tides in their natural habitat, they come to life in the current when the big generators start rolling, and the banks below the dam may be crowded with fishermen casting huge lures with saltwater spinning rods. But during the low-water conditions of late summer and fall, or whenever there aren't large releases of water, fly fishing for bass can be remarkably good. The U.S. Army Corps of Engineers will gladly provide generating schedules for a few days in advance. At Sam Rayburn Dam, where I fish, they usually don't start generating until about 9 A.M. in the summer and that gives me three hours of good morning fishing before the striper fishermen show up. If they only open one gate and

the current is light, topwater fly fishing with small
streamers and divers can continue all day for visibly
feeding fish. Some tailwaters are wadeable but this
one is not, so I have to use the boat, running up to the
dam from the nearest launching ramp, several miles
downstream.

This is light tackle fishing at its finest that I
eagerly anticipate every year. The fish are almost
always on the small side, which is a good thing,
otherwise the bass fishermen would pound the water
to death. When the current starts and the stripers
show up, I finish the morning with a drift down the
river, casting dry flies to quiet places tight against the
bank. I may catch an occasional small bass that way,
along with the abundant bluegill, but largemouth bass
fishing is good only on slack water—at least in the
rivers where I fish. Even then, I find that bass in big,
deep rivers, like those in lakes, often demand unorthodox subsurface techniques.

Among fly fishers the largemouth bass has
always been held in lower esteem than the smallmouth. This attitude may be more the result of
habitat differences than any intrinsic fighting spirit or
stronger survival instinct. In the first place, fly fishers
have historically preferred to angle for insect-eating
fish that live in cool, running water, and it is natural
that they admire the smallmouth's *(Micropterus
dolomieu)* trout-like behavior. Secondly, without
benefit of the force of current, fish in stillwater don't
fight as well as those in moving water. The old
literature is replete with comparisons of the two
species and they nearly all attribute the difference in
gameness to habitat. W.J. Loudon, for example, who
spent a lifetime fishing the then wild waters of Lake
Huron's Georgian Bay, which contained good populations of both bass, was in a unique position to com-
pare the two species. He caught both largemouth and
smallmouth every day and could not discern any
noticeable difference in fighting qualities when the
fish were taken from the same water. Loudon noted
in 1910 that habitat was the key variable. Ray
Bergman, who also caught thousands of both species
in every kind of water, said any difference was "very
slight and of little importance."

I have a friend who wants to stock small-

mouth in his new lake in Oklahoma because they
"fight better." I have tried to dissuade him because
smallmouth stay deep in southern lakes and will not
be more game than largemouth in the same pond. He
thinks they will behave as they do in the river he
fishes. He's quite wrong—their preference for lower
temperatures will, at times, force them to seek the
deeper part of his lake and they will not rise to the fly
except for a short period in the spring.

Finally, the old timers did agree that the
smallmouth was a better fish for the table—firmer
and sweeter (also, most likely, a function of environment). We couldn't care less about that today, but the
food qualities of a gamefish helped determine its
stature among anglers for many generations. Today's
fly fisher may not even remember Grandpa "throwing
back" the largemouth in disgust because they
"weren't fit to eat," but it was etched on his psyche so
he goes through life with a negative and erroneous
attitude toward Mr. Bigmouth. We kill and eat a
largemouth bass occasionally and find the flesh firm,
sweet, and very tasty indeed. My mother once told
me to throw back the brown trout and bring home
only rainbows. She said the browns were "mushy"
and, therefore, a trash fish.

## BACK IN THE TIMBER

Dam constructors normally leave vast tracts of brush
and timber in both farm ponds and large reservoirs
specifically to provide bass habitat. All sunfish are
structure-oriented and the bulk of the population will
spend most of the time in these cluttered areas. At
first glance, this labyrinthian maze of stick-ups and
stumps, limbs and logs, many of them precariously
tilted at improbable angles, appears completely
inaccessible, let alone fishable. Conventional bass
fishermen rarely attempt to penetrate such a jungle
with their expensive boats and they wouldn't be
caught dead in a float tube. Only the finny residents
on the edge of the watery thicket will ever see their
lures. With patience and persistence, however, the
tubing fly fisher can squeeze and wriggle his way into
virgin waters where bass may have never seen a
lure or fly.

For many years, I too was satisfied to stay on

the edges of the thicket but one morning the splashy rises of feeding bass, about a hundred yards back in the timber, was just too alluring. I had to try it! My fins got hung up in limbs; the tube repeatedly wedged between stumps; I encountered enormous, partially-buoyant logs that blocked my progress for 50 feet in each direction. I eased along a narrow, open channel that led toward the feeding bass, only to find it hopelessly blocked far short of the target area. Realizing that my anger and muttered expletives were not helpful, I finally regained my composure and slowly meandered through the timber, raising my legs to slip over logs and pulling the tube by hand through tangles of limbs, until I was in casting position. My first cast took a fat little 14 incher. I smugly began to false cast for another presentation but forgot where I was and my back cast snagged the rotting remnant of a pine tree. I yanked the large Dahlberg loose which fell to the water, along with a great quantity of rotten wood and debris, and it instantly disappeared down the gullet of another hungry bass. I couldn't spin the tube around quickly enough and he wrapped the tippet around the same tree that I had snagged. I took a dozen bass in the next hour and lost as many more, including all the "good" ones.

One must plan the backcast trajectory on every presentation and be able to execute the cast with little margin for error. Needless to say, an efficient weedguard is a must and many flies will be lost in any case. The barb should always be crimped and stainless hooks must never be used in any freshwater environment.

The olive/natural diver compartment in my box was empty when I decided to explore more of the jungle and practice my newly found tubing techniques. I began to develop new skills. I learned that many of those barriers are less ominous than they appear. The huge logs are only slightly buoyant and will sink at a touch to allow passage and many rotten stick-ups will crumble before the advancing tube. My worries about ripped waders never materialized; the lightweight nylon is tougher than waterlogged wood but will not, of course, withstand the remnants of barbed wire fences that are common in man-made impoundments.

I also discovered that some dead trees are so weakened at the water line that they may come crashing down with the slightest contact. The sensation of unknown, submerged objects rubbing against your legs is disquieting at first, especially in alligator habitat, but the danger is more imagined than real. Rotting brush normally breaks off just below the water line and, until I learned to move slowly, the backward movement of the tube was occasionally arrested by—I'll try to be delicate—an uncomfortable indignity of a very personal nature. I also watch for wasp's nests, another good reason for moving slowly, and try not to surprise a basking cottonmouth, both of which are common in this fascinating ecosystem. I am finding that, with practice and patience, I can maneuver the tube in many of these flooded labyrinths and present my phony offering to a completely unsuspecting Mr. Bigmouth—who has, I might add, all the odds stacked in his favor!

## OVER THE MOSS

Enormous fields of lily pads, vast beds of coontail moss, hydrilla, parrot-feather, milfoil, hyacinth and several other common water plants (collectively called "moss" in Texas) cover thousands of acres of southern reservoirs. Imported hydrilla has effectively choked off many marinas and has been the source of considerable controversy between fishermen and recreational boaters. These weed beds provide superb bass habitat and are likely responsible for the dramatic improvement in Texas bass fishing in recent years. Unlike lily pads, which are confined to shallower areas of the lake, hydrilla thrives at depths up to 15 feet and the beds may cover many square miles. These areas are only accessible to the bass boats during the winter and early spring when the plants are dormant, or when flood conditions raise the water level above the foliage, but the best fishing is in mid summer when fish congregate below the moss to beat the heat and take advantage of the abundant food. Like lily pad fields, the bottom is alive with aquatic insects, various salamanders and other amphibians, baitfish and crustaceans. If a brown trout could survive there, it would weigh thirty pounds in a few years.

Dense, living vegetation cannot be penetrated

with a float tube, but my inflatable Kikk Boat will
negotiate the beds unless the lake is very low and the
moss is hopelessly matted. A fly fisher who makes the
effort will find popping bug heaven in the small
pockets of open water scattered throughout the bed.
Unlike lily-pad fields, where the open pockets are
consistent, "holes" in the hydrilla vary with the lake
level and may change daily. When the lake rises
suddenly, the whole bed may be covered by a foot or
two of water and a Dahlberg Diver worked over the
top of the weeds is deadly. Flooded moss, however, is
also accessible to the big boats.

There is always a narrow strip of open water
along the inside edge of the weeds, next to the bank,
and bass hide in the hydrilla in order to ambush the
minnows and juvenile sunfish that frequent the
exposed shallows. Unfortunately, getting within
casting distance of the bank may require a mile of
strenuous effort. I occasionally see a powerful boat
cross the moss at high speed, but such incidents
usually occur during those high-dollar tournaments
and I tend to avoid the lake at these times. Bass
fisherman tell me that I can run my boat across dense
hydrilla if I hit the bed wide open and keep the boat
on plane. I admit that I've tried that, but my thirty-
horsepower motor is apparently too small—moss
builds up on the propeller, the boat slows down and
the motor gets hot. After a hefty repair bill, I decided
to stay with my Kikk Boat. When hydrilla blocks a
launching ramp, boat traffic will cut a lane through
the bed. The lane itself is good popping bug water on
uncrowded weekdays but be careful—the bass boats
run through this stuff wide open to keep their propellers from fouling.

Nearly all the pressure is on the outer edge of
the weed bed and, like flooded timber, the interior
remains relatively unfished. I know some bass fishermen who use a heavy slip sinker that will take a
plastic worm right through the moss to the waiting
fish below but, of course, I can't do that with my fly
rod. If the fly fisher has the persistence to develop
the requisite skills, a lot of patience and the right
equipment, he can penetrate the most remote reaches
of these vast weed beds and enjoy some incredible
angling. Pulling the Kikk Boat through the hydrilla

with a paddle can be quite a workout.

Although some weed beds may be accessible from the bank, a power boat is required equipment on large impoundments. I usually carry either a float tube or a Kikk Boat in the power boat; sometimes I carry both. It is not possible to get in and out of a float tube in deep water (although I once boarded a boat in open water—tube and all—after a close encounter with a ten foot alligator) but my Kikk Boat is quite stable and easily boarded from the anchored boat. I try not to venture more than about ten minutes away from my boat and I watch for thunderstorms.

Water hyacinth is far more insidious than other water vegetation. It forms large, drifting rafts that extend well above the surface. If solid, it does indeed effectively close off the area to fishing since it cannot be penetrated with any kind of craft and no amount of lead will take a lure through it—you can almost walk on the rafts, as birds, small mammals and reptiles actually do. The water beneath the hyacinth provides excellent habitat for bass, which are completely safe from anglers because we can't get to them. Early in the season, however, or in the presence of wind or current, the hyacinth can be accessed via constantly changing navigable channels that wind through the floating rafts. A bass boat can also negotiate these channels with the

*Hyacinth is constantly moving.*

electric trolling motor, of course, but not the "lakes" that may be formed within an encircling boundary of hyacinth. Such enclosures can remain inaccessible for weeks. I keep my eye on these places because I know that bass have gathered within the ring of vegetation to escape summertime fishing pressure.

Sometimes, I even see rising fish and have desperately tried to hack my way through the stuff, or to pull the rafts aside, but it's too heavy and thick. (Sticking your hands into hyacinth is also a good way to get bitten by a snake.) I check the area after a change in the lake level, a violent thunderstorm or flood conditions, and if an opening has been created, I feel that adrenalin rush of excitement because I know these places are normally unreachable.

I have been lost in the hyacinth more than once and have spent hours finding my way back out. The opening may close behind me on a windy day or I may find that the channels have changed. I don't lose my sense of direction in this case, because I can see the sun and the lake shore, but after hours of concentrating on the fishing, winding around in the maze, I may find that I have forgotten where the openings were. Tired and ready to go home, I may kick my tube along a channel for thirty minutes only to encounter a dead end. Being "lost" is quite un-nerving to most people, but I've gotten used to it. I get more or less lost in these forests, swamps, thickets and creek bottoms on a regular basis. Darlene knows that I will eventually find my way home and she doesn't worry anymore.

## BEHIND THE WILLOWS

Most southern reservoirs have "secondary shorelines" during the spring spawning season when lake levels are high. Lines of willows and other brush form dense barricades between the shallows and the main lake where the bass can consummate their annual tryst without human intrusion—at least until we float tubers show up. I have mixed feelings about casting to spawners, but if the fish is quickly released, and not carried all day in a live well to some distant tournament weigh-in, it will return to the nest none the worse for wear. The bass fisherman tears his hair out when big bass are spawning behind the willows.

He can hear the nest builders splashing back there but he can't get to them. One energetic fellow actually cleared a path through the thicket with a chain saw so he could reach the spawners the following spring. It didn't work—the water proved to be too shallow for his boat and wading or tubing never occurred to him. I know where the slot is, though, and I slip through it in my tube every spring, carefully piling dead brush to conceal the opening when I leave.

Exploration of any impoundment will reveal many such areas that are closed to boats, but are still flooded during the high water that normally coincides with the prime spring season. The shallows behind lines of vegetation are perfect for the tubing or wading fly fisher. I know a place, for example, in the backwaters of the Angelina River in East Texas where the only access to a large, shallow "oxbow" lake is a narrow space between two ancient cypress trees. I have to partially deflate the Kikk Boat and push it between the trees on its side, and literally go swimming to get my body through. Once on the other side, I reinflate the craft by mouth and have a ball with bass and bream that are only molested during my occasional intrusions into the hidden lake. This area looks wadeable but I have learned that wading can be dangerous business in southern waters. The bottom may be perfectly hard but suddenly change to soft, quicksand-like mud. Each advancing step must be carefully tested before putting your weight on that lead foot. When I do get stuck in the mud I am admittedly delighted to see
even a big bass boat.

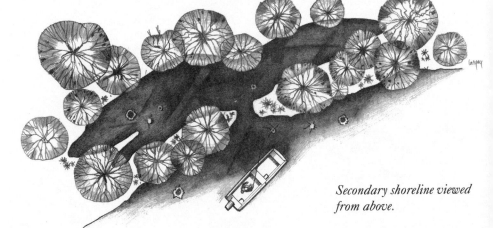

*Secondary shoreline viewed from above.*

48

We may not have these areas to ourselves for long. Several bass men have recently asked me where I bought my float tube and how much it cost. That's all right though—as long as they don't bring that big boat in there, I welcome their company. Who knows, if we get them into tubes maybe they'll even try the fly rod some day.

### TAG FISHING FOR BASS

Although it is impossible to land a bass that may be hooked in some of these brushy, weed-choked areas, we can still cast to such fish with a tactic that is gaining in popularity on catch-and-release trout waters. It's about time that trout fishers discovered what John Betts calls "pointless" fly fishing. I have been "touch-and-go" (tag) fishing for a number of years in badly cluttered habitat and also on small, private ponds where I do not want to impact the fishery. When someone is kind enough to allow fishing privileges on his choice, carefully-managed private water, the last thing one wants to do is to injure his fish in any way.

I commonly see signs of fish way back in a mass of flooded timber or thick brush—places that are quite impossible to fish with any conventional angling technique. In such a case, I simply break the hook point off the fly, round it a little with the hook sharpening file, and cast it right into the thicket. I am often rewarded with a spectacular, explosive take and, if I'm lucky, the breathtaking jump of a big bass. This is very thrilling and rewarding, nearly as much as actually landing the fish. Moreover, the experience is not marred by feelings of guilt because I haven't hurt him a bit. Don't break off too much of the hook, though, because you will change the center of gravity of the bug and it will float "belly up." Rather than breaking the point off, the hook can also be bent until the point touches the shaft, making any kind of retention impossible. In that case, however, the bug will be immediately rejected and there will be no jump—especially if a hard-body popper is used. A wide gap "stinger" hook is easier to bend than a sproat-style hook.

The bass will usually hold onto a deer-hair bug long enough to get the desired leap, or at least

*Tag fishing rigs
for both casting
and fly rod use.*

49

allow a brief look at the fish as it rolls. The rise alone is thrilling, to be sure, but it's nice to see how big the fish is. It may well be that fish in extremely cluttered habitat may have never seen a lure, or at least not for a long time. "Tag" fishing would seem truly "pointless" to most people. But this is a fun way to enjoy good fishing on even the most crowded of public lakes. In fact, all the really good fish may be in the tightest cover. Be sure to tell nearby anglers what you are doing so they will not be tempted to cast a lure in there and needlessly kill a fish. Ignore the funny looks; it's their loss.

A small plastic worm also works very well for tag fishing, if you bend the hook all the way over until the point touches the shank. It's helpful to use one pair of pliers to hold the hook firmly and another pair to bend it. There is no way for the fish to get hooked if this is done properly, and the worm cannot come-off while casting. Make a channel through the worm at home, with a dubbing needle, and then thread the eye of the tag hook into the preformed hole. The bass will hold onto this soft bait for a considerable time, reluctant to turn loose of it. You can actually get a pretty good fight from the fish, along with the adrenalin rush that John Betts says he misses, and you can quick release the fish at will by simply yanking the hook out of its mouth. It is important keep some strain on the line at all times to prevent the bass from swallowing the bait. Even if the bait is swallowed and the fish landed, it is still possible to carefully pull the bent hook out of his gullet. For this reason, it is best to use the bending method and a heavy tippet if you want to preclude any chance of damage to the fish. The worm is also less likely to hang between limbs or get wedged in the crotch of a tree than the bug or diver.

I often "tag" fish with the casting rod in order to more efficiently search for concentrations of fish. A standard 3/8 ounce spinner bait works very well for this if the barb is completely crimped. The heavy jig will immediately fall right out of the fish's mouth the moment you throw even the slightest amount of slack in the line. In this case, I have the option of either landing the fish or quick-releasing him. This cannot be accomplished with the fly rod, of course, since it

requires a heavy lure and a very large hook. The
casting rod is a vital searching tool and the fly fisher
who refuses to use it, or has failed to master it, will be
severely handicapped, especially on large lakes.

## FINDING FISH IN BIG WATER
*"Remember that even the most skillful guide will not show
to advantage on unfamiliar water . . . you have all the
opportunity to learn a lake near you."*
                                    *Jason Lucas, 1947*

It is imperative that, as I point out in *The
Sunfishes*, the serious bass fisher concentrates on one
lake and learns it thoroughly. It is frequently said that
ninety percent of the bass are taken by ten percent of
the fishermen. That ten percent consists, of course, of
regular anglers who know the bottom contours of the
reservoir. Old buildings, bridges, roadways and creek
channels are all important habitat. Bass fishers refer to
these features with names like "Church Steps," "The
Junk Yard," and "Mackenzie's Ridge." If you are
serious about bass fishing you need to know where
the structures are, and you can only gain such local
knowledge by regularly fishing the same lake. Those
who know the lake catch fish regardless of the crowds
because they know where to fish, while most week-
enders do not.

Make friends of, and try to go fishing with,
the local bass fishermen. This can be a problem for
many fly fishers, who tend to live in urban areas and
travel in very different circles. A big lake can intimi-
date a fly fisher who is used to small ponds and trout
streams. This is, in fact, the most common obstacle I
encounter in trying to encourage warmwater tyros to
try these fisheries. If you are serious about learning a
given lake, one of the bass-fishing regulars can save
you years of study. It is well worth the effort to
cultivate those kinds of relationships. Or, if you don't
know any bass fishers, you can hire a professional
guide for a few days—preferably at different times of
the year—who works on the lake you want to learn.
Guides who specialize in fly fishing are nonexistent
on these lakes, but you can still learn from a good
guide. While in the guide's boat, it's best to fish with
the casting rod and take notes surreptitiously. The

casting rod may not be your favorite way to fish, but proficiency with it is a prerequisite to success in this environment.

Hang around local tackle shops and listen to the jargon, join in the bull sessions at the launching ramp and generally make an effort to acquire information about the lake. Wherever people gather, cliques are sure to form and these lakes are no exception. Success on large, public waters is an insider's game and that's why, of all the thousands of people that fish big impoundments, only a few regulars really catch very many fish. Bass are found only in a tiny percentage of that vast expanse of water and you have to fish often to consistently do well—and having the right connections doesn't hurt.

Some bass fishermen even a install a CB radio in the boat, using prearranged codes to inform their buddies when they find good fishing. You may not care to get involved in all that, but one thing is for sure: You can never be a good bass fisher if you don't concentrate on one lake.

Bass fishers have their own organizations and rarely join fly fishing clubs. The schism that exists between the two groups is partly cultural and socio-economic, but the Bass Anglers Sportsmans Society and the Federation of Fly Fishers share many common values and conservation goals. It would be healthy for all parties if we could close this gap a bit. The main obstacle to such a coalition is not the kind of tackle we use or even differences in educational or cultural backgrounds. It is rather the bass fishers continuing devotion to organized fishing competition, especially the big money prizes and professionalism, that flies in the face of the historical values associated with the pastime of fly fishing. Nevertheless, the modern bass fisherman is dedicated to catch and release and his conservation credentials are just as good as ours. I am noticing a disturbing increase in the number of fly fishing competitions around the country, and the world, in recent years. I hope that gap isn't closing in this manner.

Fly fishers accept all sorts of space-age technology when it comes to rods and reels, lines and fly tying materials, yet rebel at any sort of electronic equipment or gadgetry that can help them under-

stand the subsurface habitat. Reading the water
visually is an important fly fishing skill, but I am
afraid we'll have to restrict that to the trout stream
and farm pond. An electronic depth finder is required
to read the water in a big lake—one reason, I suppose,
why fly fishers have always avoided big lakes. Without knowledge of bottom contours and structure, the
lake appears to be all the same—just a huge expanse
of water without character or features, almost like the
ocean. But nothing could be farther from the truth. A
depth finder brings the lake to life, reveals all sorts of
interesting features and allows you to "map" the
bottom. I don't use it to "find fish" per se, but rather
to locate structure, high spots, creek channels and
other characteristics of good habitat. Because it is
imperative to understand bottom structure to consistently catch bass, the only alternative to the electronic
depth finder is a nineteenth century lead line. Heaving a paraffin-tipped lead on a knotted line may
sound like fun, but who has that kind of time?

All your work will be wasted if you don't keep
a good record. While many trout fishers keep a diary,
it is usually as much for amusement as edification. On
these waters, however, the log book is vital for future
reference.

*Typical page from
the author's log book.*

Carefully enter all the details of each location you fish. A small, portable tape recorder is handy here, and the data can be entered on your computer when you get home. Indicate exact location, date and time of day, weather conditions, water temperature, what flies and techniques did or didn't work and what the fish seemed to be feeding on. Data like water clarity, salient bottom features, the amount of and species of vegetation present, the level of fishing pressure that day and any secondary forage sources that may be present anywhere in the water column can prove invaluable later, especially if you enter the data on a computer. Don't skip details. Their relevance may not be apparent until you reflect on the outing later at home.

There is a very fine book that covers all this in great detail: *Practical Bass Fishing* by Bill Dance and Mark Sosin. This work, illustrated by Dave Whitlock, was published nearly twenty years ago and I have just recently discovered it. I have never seen a better discussion of the importance of structure in serious bass fishing and if you intend to take advantage of these fisheries it should be on your book shelf. Reading bass fishing literature (books and magazine articles) will help you understand what kind of water bass prefer. You will learn, for example, that largemouth bass normally stay in water less than eight feet deep and seek the depths only when required to do so by uncomfortable temperature, lack of food or insufficient oxygen. There is even a chapter on fly fishing for bass. Bill Dance, in addition to being one of the all time tournament greats and a major television personality, is also a proficient fly fisher. Roland Martin and Bill Dance admit that it's a fun way to fish, but not, they emphasize, the most efficient. Martin has said that he prefers the fly rod whenever he goes fishing just for the fun of it. How many fly fishers can claim equal competence with a casting rod?

The casting rod is a more efficient tool in searching for fish. You have immediate access to the entire water column and, with a spinner bait, you can really cover a lot of water quickly. Once you locate an area of fish, you can switch to the fly rod—but you've got to find them first. If you are going to fish big water successfully, you must try to be versatile. As

long as you adhere to the catch-and-release ethic,
you're certainly not compromising any values in
switching to the casting or spinning rod when conditions demand it. As a matter of fact, conventional
methods are easier on the fish. They land fish more
quickly, are less likely to suffocate fish that become
tangled in the weeds, and fewer fish are gut-hooked.
While the fly rod is not more "sportsmanlike" than
the casting rod, it is, of course, a lot more fun. No fly
fisher really enjoys conventional tackle; cranking fish
in on a winch is not very rewarding. When I catch a
bass on casting gear my first reaction is regret that I
wasn't fly fishing. A fish caught on hardware just
doesn't mean anything to me. Nonetheless, heave-
and-crank methods are vital when it comes to
finding fish.

Without confidence and assurance that I am
working over fish, I have difficulty maintaining my
motivation. The best way to locate bass in big, deep
water is to fish likely areas with a casting rod and a
plastic worm, switching to the fly rod when you find
them. You can take some bearings on the spot and fly
fish there all weekend. If, for example, a bottom-
crawling worm produces a few small bass under a
certain moss bed at 10 A.M., the same bed may be
popping-bug heaven at dusk. You may also feel
"bream bumps" on the deep worm, indicating the
possible need for a 5-weight outfit and a box of dry
flies when you return in the evening. Fish that will
take only a worm at mid-day may feed on the surface
at dawn and dusk.

Practicing tournament fishermen often "tag"
fish with the casting rod to avoid traumatizing the
bass and spoiling the spot. They don't want to actually catch the fish at that time; they just want to know
where it is. So, they search for bass with no hook in
the worm or, rather, by crimping it over. They just
feel the strikes, and many of them are experienced
enough to even approximate the size of the fish they
are "touching." I either bend the hook as described
earlier or file the hook point until it's rounded and
dull, and then just ease the worm away from the fish
(which is often surprisingly stubborn about giving it
up). I've had the same fish repeatedly strike all the
way to the boat! Guides also fish this way on their

days off, thereby locating lunkers for future clients without spoiling the spot for them. I would be offended if a guest on my farm ponds or a companion on a trout stream suddenly broke out a casting rod, but on these big Texas impoundments the fly fisher should be able to fish both ways.

Another way I find fish is to "drift a worm" across the flats or some other likely habitat. This is very boring and no fun at all, but I'm not looking for fun. I'll have fun later with my fly rod after I find the bass. This is simply a matter or putting enough lead on the worm to hold the bottom while you let the boat drift with the wind. When I catch a fish or feel a take, I start the trolling motor and go back over the spot, casting the worm all around the area. If I do indeed determine that there is a quantity of bass there, I switch to the fly rod and start having fun. If there is no wind, I may also troll a worm, jig or spinner. That's even more boring than drifting, but I can cover a lot of water that way. Remember, I only have to resort to this occasionally. When I find a concentration of bass I can often fly fish there for several days, or sometimes even weeks, in a row. I must, however, be able to find my way back to the fish.

## TAKING BEARINGS
Lakes like Sam Rayburn in Texas, Lanier in Georgia, Bull Shoals, or those in the Tennessee Valley are enormous and require the same piloting skills used in saltwater boating.

If your lake is connected to the Mississippi, St. Lawrence or Intracoastal systems by locks, navigational charts are available from the U.S. Coast and Geodetic Survey. Since my home lakes are not connected to any navigable waterways, I do not enjoy that advantage, but the Army Corps of Engineers can provide topographical maps of many lakes that serve nearly as well for our purposes. Radar, radio direction finding, satellite navigation and other modern technology have made visual piloting obsolete, but because float tubes and jon boats are rarely equipped with Loran, the angler must depend on old-time cross bearings to "fix" his position on the featureless surface of a large lake. By carefully recording the bearings in a log book, it's easy to return to precisely the same spot on subsequent outings.

Let's suppose you are running across your home lake, far from shore, at half speed with your depth finder on. The bottom is flat, about 20 feet deep. Suddenly, the screen shows strong echoes as the bottom appears to rise to ten feet and then abruptly falls back to the original, featureless, 20-foot depth. You turn around, idle across the spot, and the depth finder reveals what is likely a mass of old, dead brush and trees that were piled up by a bulldozer when the lake was built. You anchor the boat within a comfortable casting distance of the brush pile and begin fishing an unweighted nymph on a sink-tip line. You connect with a husky bluegill on the first cast and enjoy good bream fishing all afternoon, along with several small bass and a couple of bigger fish that snapped the 4X tippet. As dusk approaches, you break out the 8-weight and big hairbugs, eagerly anticipating the topwater action that is sure to follow during the final hour of the day. But first, before darkness falls, you must stop fishing long enough to take a set of bearings so you can return to this "honey hole" (as we say in Texas) next weekend.

Open your log book to a new page. Enter the date and assign a name to the spot such as "ten-foot brush pile off Smith Marina." Then, from where you are anchored, scan the bank for prominent features— buildings, lone trees, rock faces—and find two features that line-up with each other and draw them in the book in the following manner:

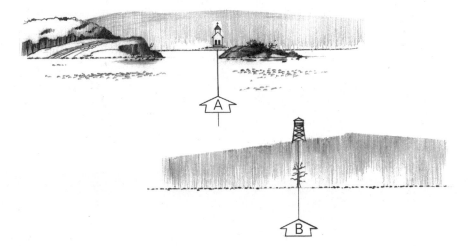

Next find two additional objects that also line up and draw that line in the same way. This second bearing should be a minimum of forty-five degrees in any direction, but not more than 135 degrees, from the first set of objects. The intersection of the two lines fixes the exact position of the brush pile. Be sure to describe the objects in detail in case your memory fails later.

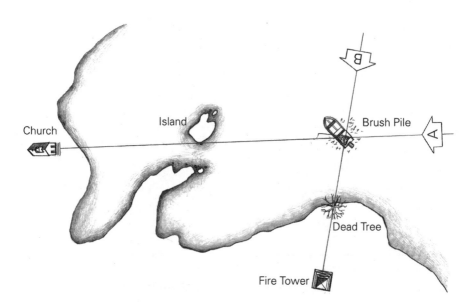

Put the log book in a safe, dry place and enjoy the evening rise with topwater flies. When you return to the lake the following weekend, consult your notes as you run to the general locale of the brush pile. Look for either of the two sets of objects and get one set in line. Then, visually locate the other set of two prominent objects. Put the first set in the middle of the stern of your boat and, keeping them in exact line, run slowly until the second set also lines up. When both sets are in line you are very close to the brush pile, probably within a hundred feet or so. Crisscross the immediate area until you see the pile on the depth finder. After you do this a few times you could find the spot in your sleep. The basic principle of cross bearings is also useful to pinpoint specific spots when fishing a small pond from a float tube,

such as a submerged spring or the top of a big stump
where bluegill spawn.

I learned this technique as a boy from commercial fishermen on the Pacific Coast and had no
idea that it was even known to freshwater anglers.
While reviewing old bass fishing literature, I discovered that both John Alden Knight and Jason Lucas
used visual bearings on open water fifty years ago,
and Lucas even describes how to widely circle another boat in order to get the bearings for the other
fellow's spot. Lucas was very competitive in his
fishing and was the father of modern bass fishing.

Returning to a particular spot along the bank
may also require some notes. I find that keeping track
of running time is often very helpful. If I want to
return to that fallen tree where I caught all the crappie last April, I simply consult my notes for that date
and find that, when I finished fishing and started
back to the launching ramp, it took me exactly eight
minutes, at normal running speed, to reach the buoy
line off the swimming beach at Smith Point. I then
run eight minutes down the bank from Smith Point to
find the fallen tree (the shape of which I have drawn
in my notes so I can distinguish it from other fallen
trees). If the crappie were spawning there last April,
they will likely be there every year at that time.
Running time also helps me negotiate the twisting
channels and bayous of the cypress swamp. For
example, when I enter the bayou from the main river
channel, I make my first turn in eleven minutes; I
turn to the right and find the nearly invisible cut that
accesses Moon Lake in precisely four more minutes
at half speed. If I run for five or six minutes, I know I
have passed the cut and must turn around and search
for it. Fluctuations in water level dramatically change
the appearance of the shoreline. Dead trees rot and
fall and floods often wash away some salient land-
mark. Running time may be the only reference I have
after a flood. In time, of course, you get so familiar
with the area that you'll no longer have to consult
your notes —but it's still a good idea to have them
handy. Learning how to take bearings can make all
the difference on bigger waters. Your log book will
gradually fill with such entries and you will eventually
commit them to memory.

Few bass fishers carry a compass but, because of my seafaring background, I am uncomfortable without one. Simple course and time is the most basic form of dead reckoning navigation, but remember that the compass will not be accurate unless it is professionally compensated. Because of the magnetic effects of nearby metal and electrical equipment on the compass, you cannot assume that, since you ran southeast to reach this point, its reciprocal, northwest, is necessarily the direction back to the launching ramp. Unless you change the position of metallic objects or electrical equipment, however, your compass will always read the same and the courses you enter in your notes will be reliable—but only on your compass, not on someone else's.

You are probably not the only one who has discovered the brush pile off Smith Point and you may return one day to find another boat fishing there. Courtesy, which is too often ignored on bass lakes, as well as on trout streams, demands that you fish elsewhere until the first fisherman leaves. You may also learn, as you get to know the other regulars on your home lake, that the brush pile has a real name - probably something like "Deacon's Pasture." Later on, on some tough, hot summer day, that bass fisherman to whom you showed due courtesy may whisper "Deacon's" in your ear as you wait in line to launch your boat. You and he may anchor on either side of the pile and both fish the spot; maybe even sharing lunch and other fishing "secrets." The next time you meet him at the launching ramp, he may suggest that you park your boat and fish with him that day.

Chances are that you will learn more about catching bass that one day than from all the books you have ever read. If you don't push the fly rod down his throat, as I unfortunately tended to do in my early days in the South, he may even develop an interest in fly fishing. Present the fly rod as simply an enjoyable alternative when the fish are on top. Let him discover the aesthetic and spiritual aspects for himself.

I once asked a successful tournament bass fisherman how he approaches a strange lake that he has never fished before, since the rules only give him a couple of practice days before the tournament. How could he possibly learn the lake in such a short time?

His answer was simple: "I watch the locals."

There is more to finding bass in big water than just locating structure. The fish migrate from deep to shallow water as conditions change, and the habitat that they occupy depends upon a number of seasonal, weather, and solunar factors, as well as on the peculiar characteristics of the bass himself. We'll take a look at some of those factors and characteristics in the next chapter.

# THREE

# YOU SHOULD'VE BEEN HERE YESTERDAY

*". . . bass fishing is quite confusing and inconsistent. There
are times when they cannot be coaxed to strike anything, and
the trip becomes a blank. At other times, they can be cap-
tured by the crudest tactics known to angling."*

*Jim Gasque, 1946*

### FEAST OR FAMINE

On the afternoon of February 2nd, Ground Hog Day,
1989, I experienced the hottest, wildest freshwater
fishing that I've ever seen (before or since)! I had
seen hundreds of hot saltwater bites, when fish took
any offering the instant it hit the water. I had also
seen evening caddis hatches on the Henry's Fork
when you couldn't keep the gulpers off the line, but I
was unaware that freshwater gamefish are capable of
the kind of feeding frenzy that I saw that memorable
afternoon.

The weather had been balmy for several days,
with temperatures in the 80s and high humidity—
more like May than January. Soaked with perspiration
from tilling the vegetable patch, I sat down in the
shade of the live oak tree, opened a can of soda and
turned on the portable radio. The local station reported that a record-breaking Siberian Express
loomed just over the horizon. Longview, a hundred
miles to the north, had already dipped into the single
digits and, the announcer continued, we could expect
the temperature to suddenly plummet in a few hours.
I knew that bass fishing is usually good before an
advancing cold front, so I forgot about the garden,
grabbed my float tube and rod and walked to the five-
acre pond across the road. I was not prepared for what
I found.

The heavily-fished little lake, which normally
yields only a couple of small bass and a few bream on

a typical outing, was alive with feeding fish. Nice bass, slab crappie (which always hold deep) and huge bluegills were smashing the size-4, yellow popper on every cast. They were behaving like a school of Spanish mackerel chasing baitfish! I lost count, of course, but I completely wore out several high-quality cork bugs in two hours. I must have released 50 fish— more than I dreamed existed in this "fished-out" pond. I stayed in the water until the advancing mass of arctic air dissolved this halcyon day with an ominous line of rolling thunder. The big pine tree by the pier was whipping violently and the dirty sky was ablaze with lightning when I released my last fish, a beautiful eighteen incher. I sloshed home without noticing the cold rain and spent the evening tying flies beside a roaring fire, basking in that glow of satisfaction that every angler knows.

If I had to describe warmwater fishing in a single phrase, it would be "feast or famine." It is a common experience to catch dozens of bluegills and bass in a given pond and return the next day to find dead water. Sometimes I can attribute these extremes to an obvious weather change, water temperature or to the presence or absence of feed, but, as often as not, the reasons are quite inexplicable. Warmwater species are more inclined to feed heavily at certain times rather than nibbling all day as trout do. A stream trout cannot afford to let a drifting natural pass him by, but these warmwater fish enjoy a more extensive menu and the food forms that are available to them tend to be larger and more substantial. It takes a lot of *Baetis* nymphs to equal the protein content of one 12-inch water snake! A four-pound bass can gorge itself with an hour of effort whenever it chooses, but trout must forage constantly in all but the very richest of coldwater habitats. The trick, then, is to learn to anticipate when bass will choose to feed.

Tomes have been written in an effort to explain bass behavior in terms of subtle changes in weather, atmospheric pressure, water chemistry, water temperature, phases of the moon, solar factors and even the position of the Zodiac. I haven't begun to understand, let alone apply, all that data. I have, however, developed a sort of gut feeling, an educated guess if you will, that tells me when to go fishing . . .

or more accurately, when not to go. I think I too respond to atmospheric pressure, because on a good fishing day I get a kind of "heavy," even oppressive, feeling. Fly fishing is best when the weather is sticky, muggy, clammy, overcast and dead still. But the only absolute rule that I can count on is that the fish will never bite when I have an important guest. It is frustrating when I entertain trout-fishing friends who do not understand that bass and other sunfish often "pig out" and then remain inactive for several days. Nor is this something new. Jim Gasque writes of an angling experience in his 1946 book, *Bass Fishing*, to which I can really relate. It seems that Gasque had invited a group of fly fishers on a bass-fishing trip to his most productive water, North Carolina's Lake Adger. The party of five never saw a bass all day and Gasque was devastated. Despite the efforts of the gracious Mrs. Robert Dowtin, a prominent lady angler of the time, to assuage his feelings, he was embarrassed to the point of physical illness. "For some time, a mental cloud hovered over me as a result of this experience," he wrote. Gasque recognized, a half-century ago, that a deeper offering would likely have produced a few fish, "although it is not so interesting as fishing near the surface."

## AS THE SEASONS CHANGE

During the prime spring season, each passing cold front spoils fishing for a couple of days. Many bass fishermen attribute this strictly to the cooling of the surface water, but the notion that weather is significant only as it affects water temperature is an over-simplification. Weather changes introduce many other factors into the equation. I am convinced that a sudden change in barometric pressure is the main culprit. Sometimes the front is quite minor, and the drop in either air or water temperature may scarcely be perceptible, but the fish still turn off with rising pressure. One thing is for certain: once the front passes you can "hang it up" for awhile. Recovery time depends on the strength of the system. Stiff northerly or easterly winds on the heels of a powerful cold front will spoil the fly fishing for several days. As the weather warms and the barometer stabilizes, spring-time fishing will improve daily and peak when the pressure again begins to fall during the hours before the next front arrives. Fish go berserk as the barometer falls and my predatory instincts are also aroused by that sultry, still, heavy feeling that precedes these fronts. It excites me in a frighteningly primitive, almost lustful, sort of way. Nothing can keep me off the lake at such times—well almost nothing. They tell a story in East Texas about a bass fisherman who stopped fishing and removed his hat as a funeral procession passed on the levee road. Another angler commented on how polite he was to make that gesture of respect. "Yup," he drawled, "we were married for over forty years."

It has been my experience that barometric pressure directly affects fish behavior. I can't tell you what the mechanism is, but I've seen it in the ocean, on the trout stream, and especially in warmwaters. Connecticut angler, Steve Tofani, has observed changes in baitfish behavior when barometric pressure is falling—they seem to concentrate in schools— and he theorizes that the changes in feeding patterns that we experience may result more from the effects of atmospheric pressure on the bass's prey than on the fish itself:

> ". . . rising pressure entrains more air and oxygen into the upper levels and shallower portions of the lake. Conversely, a dropping barometer reduces oxygen in the same lake sections. I believe that this reduction of oxygen causes all of the fish holding there, which are primarily small, forage type species, to retreat in a somewhat wobbly state to deeper, more stable water. This has been going on for millennia, and bass exploit this behavior of disoriented prey fish, which are in a very vulnerable state . . . My own experience is that bass are aggressive every time, without exception, the barometer drops— especially at the beginning of the drop."

Steve emphasizes that barometric pressure has no effect below ten feet, which seems to make sense. I had hoped that Steve's theory would offer a plausible explanation for a mystery that has bothered me since my charter-boat days. How could bottom

fish that live under terrific pressure, 300 feet deep in
the Pacific Ocean, react to barometric changes? I
know it doesn't seem possible, but Pacific rockfish
definitely react to pressure changes. Perhaps the
behavior of baitfish that Steve has observed causes
some kind of a domino effect on the food chain that
quickly works its way through the water column to
even that great depth. In any case, atmospheric
pressure is a major factor in the behavior of all fish,
and the angler should consider the barometer
when deciding whether to head for the stream,
lake or ocean.

Hurricanes have the lowest pressure of all,
and Andrew only grazed us in East Texas after it
annihilated South Florida and crossed the Gulf,
cutting a swath of devastation across neighboring
Louisiana. When it seemed to be heading our way in
Texas, prudence demanded that we prepare for the
worst. To my wife's dismay, I chose not to get ready
for severe weather, but rather went fishing during the
hours preceding the storm's arrival, to check the
effects of rapidly dropping barometric pressure. I
could always build a new house, but this fishing
opportunity would come only once! We all have our
own priorities. The fish were biting all right, but I
must admit that fly fishing, while my neighbors
nailed plywood to their windows and our high school
gymnasium filled with evacuees from Beaumont, did
appear inappropriately frivolous, even callous.
Darlene was appalled and still hasn't gotten over the
neighbor's valid observation that "your husband is a
madman."

During our prime season of March and April, I
would guess that conditions are right for fly fishing
only half the time. And even with optimum weather,
the fish don't feed all day. A number of other factors,
especially daily fluctuations of water temperature,
enter into the equation. The "feast" will likely occur
in the muggy afternoon on the day preceding the next
front, while the chilly morning after will almost
certainly be a "famine" time. While the barometer is
certainly a major factor, water temperature is still the
single most important variable. Fly fishers catch few
fish in water cooler than about 65 degrees or warmer
than about 85 degrees, but casting-rod anglers, who

can present a deeper bait, take a lot of winter fish in much cooler water. In fact, most of those fifteen-pound Texas lunkers that you read about are caught during the winter on weighted plastic worms. I know little about winter fishing—I just haven't done much of it—but my bassin' friends assure me that Tom Nixon's unorthodox techniques, especially the use of soft plastic lures, may make it possible for me to catch a giant winter bass on my fly rod, if I am willing to use a plastic worm and brave the nasty January weather.

Here in Texas, we often enjoy a couple of very balmy weeks in late January or early February, as we did in 1989, with superb fishing all day long. It's not uncommon to enjoy an extended period of lovely, spring-like weather right in the dead of winter. The shallows may warm well into the sixties, fooling the bass into thinking spring has arrived. They will begin to feed heavily in a typical pre-spawn mode and, if the weather holds for a few more days, they actually move into bedding areas and prepare to spawn. This phenomenon, what bass fishers call a "false spawn," offers the hottest bass fishing you will ever experience. Lunkers that hide at the bottom all summer will now slam a popping bug with reckless abandon. While I have seen successful spawns in February, cold weather usually returns before any actual bedding takes place, and bass repress their hormones until March.

The real spawn invariably coincides with the appearance of pine pollen in the early spring. Great quantities of powdery yellow pollen, often completely covering the water, waft from shoreside woods; when the urban angler sees this phenomenon in his own neighborhood he should call in sick and go fishing. These events occur a lot earlier than most people realize. The fly fisher should try to synchronize his schedule with nature. Too many anglers fail to visit the lake early enough in the year. If you wait until the pretty weather of April or May, you have missed the best fly fishing of the season.

There may be a feeding lull right after the spawn, while the spent fish recuperate, but they will reappear in a few days with ravenous appetites. Fishing can be quite slow during the lull. Fly fishers who do not understand the feast or famine nature of

these fisheries are completely dumbfounded when
they encounter slow fishing during the spring prime
or at other times when conditions seem perfect. A
respected Houston angler commented to me that the
Angelina River below Rayburn Dam is "dead water."
How did he arrive at that conclusion? He drifted it
one time and never got a take on his flies. That river,
like most southern and midwestern waters, is alive
with both bass and bream, but a trout fisher finds
these kinds of feeding cycles incomprehensible. It
would be impossible for a skilled angler to drift a
good trout stream, under favorable weather conditions, without getting a single strike on either drys or
nymphs, and I can understand how he could arrive at
the erroneous conclusion that there are no fish in
the river.

Bass fishers understand this. They fish a lot
more than most fly fishers do, and accept the bad with
the good. My Houston friend might have enjoyed
some action that day if he had tied a small plastic bait
to his leader but, of course, death would be preferable
to that. This attitude precludes, I'm afraid, the
offering of formal guiding services to coldwater-
oriented fly fishermen. I have been forced to accept
the reality that many, possibly most, fly fishers may
never find serious bass fishing to their liking.

Good topwater fly fishing resumes after the
spawn and continues during the gorgeous southern
spring, punctuated only by passing cold fronts, and it
doesn't slow down until the spiderworts bloom in
June. When those beautiful blue flowers greet the
dawn, bass leave the shallows but big bream start
feeling their reproductive urges.

While any sort of weather change during the
long, oppressive dog days of summer will stimulate
intense feeding activity, bass are very sluggish during
the hot summer months. As the locals say, "they get
lock jaw." The bass are still vulnerable to fly fishing
at night, however, and for a brief period in the very
early morning. I enjoy some exciting topwater fly
fishing right after dawn, but it stops as soon as the
blazing sun clears the pines on the east bank. I
normally return to the house at this point, since I live
close to the lake, because the heat becomes quite
intolerable after 10 o'clock. If you're tough enough to

continue fishing through the day, as most of my bass fishing friends are, your only feasible option is to drag a soft plastic salamander or crawfish slowly along the bottom. Afternoon thunder showers often will bring the fish back up into fly fishing range. The rain cools both the water and the air, temporarily creating comfortable conditions for fish and fisherman alike. This "bite" is very brief, and subsurface fishing conditions return with the baking sun.

The Gulf Coast generally gets a week or two of drizzly, overcast weather in mid summer. This is fly fishing heaven, when the midge larvae rise into the surface film to pupate, triggering secondary hatches of bream and minnows. Everything will be feeding at this time and you'll probably do well with any fly, anywhere in the lake. This is definitely a time of feasting. Summer fishing is usually good on calm, overcast days, due not only to cooler surface temperatures but also to lower levels of subsurface light that helps the bass conceal itself from prey. Bass ambush tactics are much enhanced by subdued light, and that's why these fish are more inclined to attack topwater offerings at dawn, dusk or under a cloudy sky. Some of my best bass fishing has been on those steaming, dreary, overcast summer days when not a breath of breeze is stirring. Such weather is less oppressive than fishing in the hot sun, despite the sticky feeling and sweat-soaked clothing, and the bass are usually actively feeding on that sort of day. Always carry plenty of drinking water in the boat when you fish under these conditions—enough to last you for awhile in case the outboard motor breaks down. Believe me, I've been there.

The first real noticeable cool front of fall passes across Dixie in September. Rather than turn fish off as in the spring, this front will stimulate heavy feeding activity for a couple of days. I think water temperature is the main factor here. The shallows have been too hot for comfortable feeding, and the bass have been sulking in deeper water. Now, with cooling conditions, bass hide in the brush, ready to charge any hapless minnow or frog that is foolish enough to show itself. The first fall front also brings on the appearance of large hoppers and giant dragon flies, both of which interest adult bass.

Although wind of any sort can stimulate
subsurface feeding, it will usually kill the topwater
action. I don't understand it, but bass are loathe to
take a bug on wind-rippled water. Maybe they can't
see it, I just don't know. I do know that you might as
well put away the box of bugs and divers when the
wind blows. A fair southerly breeze in early spring or
late fall will warm the top of the water column and
draw fish up from the cold depths. Bass fishers tell us
to fish the windward side of the lake on such breezy
days because the water will be warmer than along the
lee bank and wind-blown food items pile up against
the downwind shore. I'm sure they are right, but I
still prefer the comfort and serenity of a lee bank or a
line of trees. I don't like to fish in the wind. I spent
many years as a charter-boat captain, so I've had all
the wind I want. The northerly airs that follow a cold
front may drive fish down and create the kind of
conditions that demand deep fishing, but any easterly
wind, even a light breeze, will flat out kill the fishing.
If a steady east wind is blowing, you might as well go
home. Southerners have an old saying about this:
Wind from the East, fish bite least,
Wind from the West, fish bite best.
Wind from the North, go not forth.
Wind from the South, hook 'em in the mouth.

A stiff wind from any direction makes it very difficult
to handle the boat, casting is a nightmare, and, if the
wind comes up unexpectedly, it can also make it
dangerous to be on a large impoundment. If you fish
the big reservoirs, always keep a close eye on the
weather. I once heard a horror story about a fly fisher
who spent a night of terror in his float tube in the
middle of a large reservoir. Apparently, he was fishing
near the bank at dusk when a stiff offshore wind
came-up, and he couldn't develop enough thrust with
the fins to keep the wind from blowing him far out
into the lake. A bass boat rescued him in the morning.
I am admittedly treading on dangerous
ground in generalizing about the effects of weather, as
Dallas fly fisher, Tom Fadoir, and I discovered one
recent morning. Conditions could not have been
better—weather, water temperature, clarity—all
perfect. When we arrived, I would have cheerfully bet

my fly rod that I would take a bass within three casts.
Two hours later we were still casting without a strike;
not one hit—nothing at all! We finally went home
about noon. I learned the next day, from the chatter in
the coffee shop, that the bass started biting at 2:30
P.M. and fed heavily for two hours. Even more reveal-
ing, they fed at precisely that time on every lake in
the area. I have always ignored the solunar tables, but
I wouldn't be surprised if that afternoon activity
coincided with a predicted feeding period.

## TIME OF DAY

Tom Nixon's bassin' tactics, which we'll look at in
Chapter Five, have not only allowed me to fish all day
instead of only in the morning, and to keep up with
my "heave n' crank" companions, they have also
made night fishing much more feasible. Although
Florida guide Doug Hannon and other experts
dispute this, larger bass tend to be nocturnal—at least
in my ponds.

I've always had trouble fishing a bug or other
topwater fly in the dark. I can't see it and must strike
on the sound of the take, which usually results in a
missed strike. Also, no fly is completely weedless, and
when I can't see the cover I usually cast into it and
hang up. Contrary to conventional fly fishing wisdom,
surface fishing is much better on a dark night. I have
learned from other bass fishermen that it's more
productive to fish a sub-surface offering on a moonlit
night and a topwater bait on dark nights. I'm reluctant
to run my boat on a pitch black night, though. I'm
afraid I will hit a stump, or worse, another boat. It's
much safer to restrict your fishing on public lakes to
bright nights. My friends use a black plastic lizard
almost exclusively at night. The four-inch version of
that bait works very nicely for nighttime fly rodding.
They are absolutely weedless, far more forgiving of
casting errors and, most importantly, you react to the
feel of the strike rather than a visual take, as with a
bug or diver. Significantly, the various salamanders,
water dogs, newts and similar amphibians forage
exclusively at night, and that's when they are most
vulnerable to fish predation. A soft-plastic mud puppy
makes perfect sense at night. Tom Nixon's book
opens up not only night fishing, but lots of other

previously ignored opportunities to open-minded fly
rodders. Tom's fly rod spinner bait works better than
flies at night. If you use a jig with a fine-wire hook
and a heavy tippet, you can free it from any snag by
straightening the hook. If you pull too hard on a big
fish, of course, you can free the jig from its mouth the
same way.

Many anglers believe that daylight fishing will
be slow when the moon is full because, the theory
goes, the fish feed at night. Fishing does seem to be
slower during that lunar phase, but I wonder if it's not
a self-fulfilling prophecy. We anticipate poor fishing
so we don't try as hard and give up early. I have spent
a number of nights on the lake under a full moon,
and, frankly, I haven't noticed any extraordinary
feeding activity. In any case, it's a wonderful alibi for a
guide because everyone believes it. I would use the
full moon as an excuse on my charter boat and it
always worked!

Many serious bass fishers consult the so
tables daily and try to be on the lake during prin
periods. Studies conducted by Texas Parks and
Wildlife indicate that a statistically significant
majority of lunker bass are taken during peak
solunar periods; and Florida guide, Doug Hann
found, after studying thousands of big-bass catc
that the chances of catching a trophy are 500 percent
better within a major solunar period and 300 percent
better within a minor period.

The solunar theory was refined in the late
1920s by John Alden Knight, a highly-respected fly
fisher. (A contemporary of fly tier and master angler
Joe Messinger, Knight was a warmwater pioneer.) He
discovered that the concept of daily feeding cycles is
rooted in American Indian folklore, and was applied
with deadly effectiveness by nineteenth-century
market hunters. Along with H.E. Horne and George
Wylie, he published the tables in newspapers all over
the country and explained the theory in detail in his
1942 work, *Moon Up, Moon Down*. Had I known its
history, I might have taken the theory seriously years
ago rather than erroneously dismissing it as astrologi-
cal pseudo science. Experiences like Tom Fadoir and
I had, not to mention the conclusive findings of
Hannon and others, have converted me to a solunar

believer. Virtually every bass pro and fisheries expert with whom I have spoken has acknowledged its validity, but they hasten to add that other variables can override solunar factors.

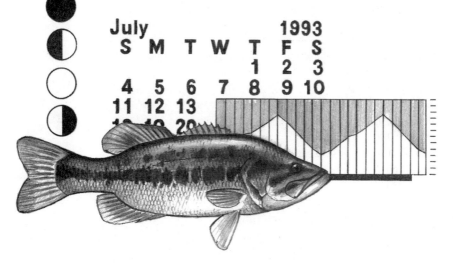

Bass tournaments are big business in Texas, and I listen to a lot of Monday morning quarterbacking. Despite the fact that they are fishing different lakes, these fellows frequently tell similar stories: "They bit early Saturday morning and nothing the rest of the weekend." "All hell broke loose right after lunch." "I couldn't buy a strike all day but limited-out just before dark." I've been hearing this for years and am always astonished that the bass seem to feed at the same time on all the lakes over a wide area.

Scientific confirmation of solunar factors now explains this. I witnessed the same phenomenon many times while fishing for Pacific salmon at sea: boats many miles apart would simultaneously experience a "hot bite." Our fleet would be strung out over thirty miles of ocean and suddenly the radio would come alive with fish reports. I did not attribute such events to solunar factors at the time, but there really isn't any other plausible explanation. Moreover, people with aquariums tell me that their goldfish seem to feed by the tables, and I have observed that periods of good fishing appear to coincide with the feeding activities of squirrels, deer and other wildlife.

The shortcoming of this system is that few

anglers are able to schedule their outings to coincide with the solunar periods, but there is still a practical application for these data. While some bass fishers will stay out on the lake all day long, most of us like to return to shore during the middle of the day to rest and cool off. We can plan our rest and fishing periods more efficiently by consulting the tables for that particular day. If there is a peak solunar period at four in the afternoon, for example, we may wish to go out earlier than usual for the evening rise or we may choose to endure the heat to take advantage of a peak mid-day period. It's amazing how quickly one forgets about uncomfortable weather when "they're biting." Whether you elect to use the tables or not, they are, like the full moon, very helpful in making credible excuses for not catching fish.

Since real fly fishing is only practicable on or near the surface, water temperatures and light levels dictate restricting topwater offerings to early morning and rainy periods during the heat of summer, and late afternoon in the cooler months of spring and autumn. The rest of the time we are better off, at least if we want to catch bass, to switch to other fly rod lures.

A number of years ago, my old friend and fellow Texan, Jimmy Nix, considered entering a major bass tournament with his fly rod. It turned out that B.A.S.S. rules prohibited the use of any rod longer that seven feet in  major tournaments, but for awhile we thought he might be able to do it. We knew that Jimmy's surface flies would give the others a run for their money under optimum weather conditions, but the odds of that were only 50/50. Our small but enthusiastic cheering section wouldn't be able to help him if the prescheduled event coincided with a "famine" solunar period or fell on the heels of a cold front. He would be wiped out! We all knew that when a bottom-crawling offering is required, even an expert like Jimmy couldn't compete with the worm-rigged casting rod. He would be forced to resort to bait casting to score at all, thereby destroying his fly fishing image forever (as I am probably doing now with such suicidal statements).

## WATER CLARITY
While I can tolerate heat, cold, wind, mosquitoes and

a host of other discomforts, I draw the line at dirty
water. I have found that real fly fishing is a waste of
time when the range of underwater visibility is less
than 18 inches. I can, however, take bass under turbid
conditions with Ron Knight's little spinner bait or
some sort of spinner-fly combo. The spinner blade is
a must in dirty water, where bugs and other topwater
baits don't work at all. You might think that a surface
disturbance would attract fish as readily as the spinner, but I think they are reluctant to attack something
that they can't see. I have noticed, under clear conditions, that bass will watch a bug for a few moments
before charging it. Bass don't seem to mind murky
water at all—in fact they thrive in it. Their eyes are
much more efficient than most baitfish and the poor
visibility makes it easier for bass to catch prey. Turbidity bothers us a lot more than it bothers them.

Tournament fishers must learn to fish in dirty
water—it's their livelihood—but I prefer to avoid it
and choose to find cleaner areas of the lake. The main
body of my home water, Lake Steinhagen on Texas's
Neches River, remains more or less muddy all year.
There are no dams for a long distance up the Neches,
so it carries a heavy load of suspended silt, which has
also filled in the lake over the years and created
severe weed problems. I've learned when and where
I can expect clear water: where creeks enter the lake,
protected coves, near the banks and, especially, in and
behind dense vegetation. Weeds serve as filters, the
suspended silt settles on them. When I shake a lily-
pad stem, clouds of dirt fill the water.

The Angelina River joins the Neches a few
miles upstream from the lake. It comes out of Lake
Sam Rayburn clean and clear and, when they are
generating with the gates wide open, it carries more
water than the Neches, providing me with a lot of
clear water to fish. If the gates are closed at Rayburn
and rainfall upstate has filled the Neches, the whole
lake can be quite turbid. I may still be able to find
clear water in certain creek channels, however, in all
but the worst of flood conditions. You must learn your
own waters so you know how to deal with various
situations. Some lakes never have turbidity problems.
Our big reservoirs—Rayburn and Toledo Bend—are
always fairly clear, but smaller waters are often

unfishable after heavy rains. Northern lakes sur-
rounded by forests and rocky terrain are also immune
to this problem, but many midwestern waters are
perpetually murky, even muddy. If your local waters
fit into the latter category, don't give up on them.
Most have populations of both bass and bream, and
it's a matter of learning how to fish them.

Farming, logging and construction on the
feeder creek will create muddy conditions when it
rains. The suspended material normally settles-out
quickly, depending on the soil type, and may even
bring needed nutrients and minerals to the lake. Too
much siltation, however, can wreak havoc with
aquatic insect life. Fortunately, most of our Texas
mayflies are burrowing species and cope quite well
with mud, unless a whole load is dumped right on top
of them. Agricultural runoff is often rich in the nutrients that, unless it's very severe, may be beneficial to
a warmwater lake or pond.

Ron Knight is an expert on fishing murky
waters and I suggest you acquire some of his fly-rod
spinner baits if you fish in midwestern lakes and
rivers. I once took Ron to a large private lake here in
Texas and I was embarrassed and horrified when I
discovered that it was literally brown with mud. Ron
wasn't perturbed in the least. He enthusiastically
strung his fly rod and tied on a very small spinner bait
with a white skirt and handed one to me. We caught
lots of small bass during the next two hours, enjoying
almost constant action. The fish were right against the
bank in mere inches of water. I didn't grasp the
significance of that until I read Rick Taylor's informa-
tive book, *Guide To Successful Bass Fishing.* As Rick
explains:

". . . the poorer the visibility, the shallower he
[the bass] will come . . . turbid water makes
bass less fearful of their enemies [and] in
murky water the baitfish also move shallower
because their food (plankton) may be nonexistent in the sunless depths. [Since] turbid
water means poor lateral visibility, a bass may
find it advantageous to be nearer the surface
where he can better see food silhouetted
against its light."

How about that? Suddenly, thanks to Taylor and Knight, it all came together and now I know where and how to fish when I can't find clean water. A spinner bait cast tight to the bank will usually scratch at least a few fish and save the day.

## WATER CHEMISTRY

Rick Taylor and his friends get very serious about things like pH and dissolved oxygen. They talk about thermoclines and oxyclines, inversions and stratifications, epilimnions and hypolimnions, and some of them even carry sophisticated instruments in their boats to check water chemistry. Fly rodders do not compete in megabucks tournaments so we don't feel the need to get that scientific about our fishing. Nonetheless, there are a few practical guidelines that every warmwater angler should follow.

I don't catch bass in the backs of coves unless there's a creek feeding the lake, especially if the water is "black." Tannin stained water, in swamp areas for instance, can be excellent bass habitat if it's oxygenated, but the combination of low oxygen and high acidity in dead back waters yields few bass. Bowfin love those areas, however, and you might want to tie-on a wire shock tippet and try for one of these ferocious fellows before leaving the cove. Avoid concentrations of dead vegetation. Decaying organic matter robs the water of oxygen and fish leave these areas.

On my home lake, the Army Corps of Engineers sprays the hyacinth with herbicide every summer in response to angler and boater complaints. Visiting anglers fish in the open holes, shortly after the hyacinth dies, because it looks like a logical place to cast. The sad fact is that there are no fish there at all because the rotting hyacinth uses up much of the dissolved oxygen. Remember that living plants produce oxygen while dead vegetation consumes it.

Fish require more oxygen to survive in warm water but, ironically, dissolved oxygen levels drop as the water heats up. Both forage fish and bass seek those areas of the lake where oxygen is the highest. That's why cooler, vegetated waters produce best in summer. Wind can also increase the dissolved oxygen in the upper levels and that's why the shallows along

the windward bank usually give-up a few bass on a
hot, blustery day.

I do not intend to carry a portable chemistry
lab in my boat, but a little common-sense understanding of pH and oxygenation in freshwater lakes can
prevent casting to empty water all day.

### SATIATED BASS

Bass, especially the big ones, don't constantly eat like
trout. They are binge feeders. They have a lot more
food available to them and tend to gorge themselves
in a burst of intense activity and then rest quietly for
hours, days or, as some bass fishermen claim, even a
week. Major emergences of aquatic insects and the
"secondary hatches" of baitfish that accompany
them—clusters of tadpoles, juvenile water snakes,
catfish fry, large numbers of hoppers or other large
terrestrials, or concentrations of shad or minnows w
all stimulate heavy feeding activity. You will be in f
fishing heaven if you're lucky enough to be on the
lake when the feast occurs, but such events invarial
are followed by a couple of days of slower fishing
while the bass rest and digest.

The enormous hatches of big *Hexagenia*
mayflies that emerge from my home lake every Jun
still drive me crazy, even though I now understand
why fishing is so slow on the second and third days
the hatch. There is something about fishing among
millions of copulating and egg-laying spinners with
out being able to induce a rise in a fish-filled lake t
will drive any fly fisher up the wall. Both bass and
bream feed so heavily on emergers during the first
day, as well as on the myriad baitfish that are thereby
drawn into open water, that they simply become
satiated and remain lethargic for some time thereafter.
This sort of thing is less common to a trout fisher and
it took me some time to understand and deal with it.
It's yet another manifestation of the feast or famine
nature of these fisheries.

*An emergence of large
Hexagenia mayflies
can sometimes
stimulate heavy
feeding by bass.*

I have found only one way to deal with
satiated bass: offer them a slow-moving, soft-plastic
lure on or near the bottom. This is yet another reason
why learning to fish with soft plastic is a must for the
serious fly rodder in bass country. It has changed my
whole fishing life. As you'll see in Chapter Five, we

don't have to switch to the casting rod anymore. We can catch 'em on the fly rod.

## CROWDED CONDITIONS

Famine conditions are often experienced on popular lakes due to heavy fishing pressure. As I indicated in Chapter One, water skiers, rock-throwing youngsters, sailboats or noisy swimmers don't seem to bother bass much. Heavy fishing pressure, however, will give them a severe case of lockjaw. Jason Lucas, a bass fishing pioneer, enjoyed the challenge of crowded, heavily-fished lakes. Anyone, he said, can catch bass on a wilderness lake but it takes a master to score on tough, popular waters. I still prefer the wilderness lake, but that's only a nostalgic memory. Most of us have to learn to fish under crowded conditions whether we like it or not (that's true on the trout stream, too).

On a crowded weekend, especially in the spring and early summer, there may be thousands of anglers on a big, public impoundment. They fish mostly along the shoreline because that's all most of them know how to do, and there is usually a steady parade of passing bass boats. One such Saturday, I was fishing a brushy area in the back of a little cove, from my tube, in the Veech Basin area of Lake Sam Rayburn. I was enjoying steady action from both small bass and white crappie. I wasn't playing by the rules, remaining in one spot like that, and boats kept coming through every few minutes in a seemingly endless line. Some would courteously stop casting and pass widely, while others went right between me and the bank, tossing their spinner baits into the cover I was fishing. Most of these people weren't catching fish, or even expecting to catch fish. They were just enjoying a pleasant day outdoors with friends and family.

I caught one or two fish between each passing boat. The action would stop with the approach of each boat, but then recover quickly after the boat disappeared around the corner of the cove, only to quit again when the next one approached. As soon as each boat left the cove I'd hook another bass or crappie. This went on all day, and absolutely convinced me that the trolling motors and lures were scaring the fish. No doubt about it. I know from experience that if these same boats had run by at 10 miles per hour with their gasoline motors, the bass would have ignored them and kept on biting. They learn which sounds are threatening and which are not. Doug Hannon's excellent video, *Understanding Big Bass*, will help you appreciate this aspect of bass behavior.

The obvious solution, of course, is to avoid public waters on the weekends. I am in a position to do that, but many anglers have to work during the week. If you live fairly close to your home lake, try it on Sunday afternoon. Most of the anglers that visit our East Texas lakes come from either Dallas or Houston, both several hours away, and head back to the city after lunch on Sunday. Sam Rayburn and Toledo Bend are deserted after three o'clock, and I've had some of my best fishing on Sunday evenings. Other anglers report that this seems to be the case on similar lakes around the country. Even Sunday morning is less crowded than Saturday, especially in the deep South where most people attend church.

If you must fish on Saturday, find less popular areas of the lake. Up river arms where the water is off color, an area served only by an old, ill-maintained launching ramp, shore lines exposed to the wind or hard-to-find high spots that rise out of deep water are all less likely to be crowded. Ask yourself where would you least want to take your family fishing and go there. Weed-choked backwaters, flooded timber, shallow areas behind "secondary" shorelines or impenetrable willows and brush—all provide refuge from the crowds.

The typical weekender will rarely venture into such areas; he feels quite dependent on his electric trolling motor and will not attempt to take his big boat into areas where he cannot use it. He is also worried about scratching or marring the paint job on his beautiful $25,000 rig; nicking the propeller on a submerged stump; getting leaves, vegetation or dirt inside the boat, and may avoid some of the best areas because duck weed or acidic water may leave an ugly stain at the waterline. As a matter of fact, the backwaters may actually be more crowded on weekdays because that's when the most serious and knowledgeable anglers fish.

If you don't like company, you may want to avoid the schools of voracious white bass that appear on big, southern lakes during the summer. The little fleet that forms around one of these schools presents quite a spectacle: kids shouting with joy, women shrieking, and dozens of fish flying into the boats. Fishing in the South is often a family, social affair. Boats tie-up in a circle for night crappie fishing. Lights, food, minnows and stories are shared and a grand time is had by all. This custom, like "dinner on the ground" and rollicking tent revivals, is a slice of Americana that will bring a nostalgic tear to the most cosmopolitan eye.

# FOUR

# THE WAY IT WAS

If you're from Dixie, you may remember Grandpa
talking about going "splat fishin'," or "spat" fishing as
Joe Brooks called it. This fishing technique was
named for the sound the bug makes when it strikes
the water. This southern style of one-handed fly
fishing, normally done from a flat-bottom boat, was a
refined "art" in the Gulf states. It flowered between
the world wars and disappeared with the introduction
of the spinning reel.

The splat fisher handled a fly rod with a short
length of line and a huge bass bug in his right hand
(unless he was left handed) and a single oar in his left.
Bracing the oar against his forearm, he propelled and
maneuvered the boat by "sculling," all the while
"splatting" something like a yellow Peck's Popper
into likely cover. This was not a crude operation. On
the contrary, it demanded exceptional coordination,
natural skill and a lot of practice. He used a stiff fly
rod (often chopping a foot off store-bought rods to be
able to both "pop" the bug and set the hook with th
rod tip while using a heavy level line). A modern
weight-forward line really wouldn't have helped
much because rarely were casts more than thirty fee
Ever wonder what those automatic reels were for?
Always boorish on a trout stream, they were a major
technological advance along the Suwanee and the
Pearl, the Calcasieu and the Neches. Grandpa could
instantly pick up loose line and get the bass tight wi
a flick of his little finger, giving time to set the oar
down and play the fish. Those that lacked the coordination and skills to splat fish, could always "jiggle" or
"skitter." The jiggler tied a lure to a six-inch leader,
which was itself attached to the end of a very long
cane pole. The tip of the pole was poked into the
weeds and the bug was jiggled. I saw people jiggling

*Automatic fly reel*

in the reeds that grow along the banks of California's Clear Lake as late as 1956. To skitter a spoon, the lure was tied to a line about equal to the length of the cane pole—usually twelve to fifteen feet—and the angler "skittered" the spoon on top of the water with sweeping motions. Joe Brooks reported that before World War II, many southern bass fell for these tactics. As one hoary-headed old boy told me: "This here weren't no Yankee fishin'."

*Splat fishin' is harder than it looks.*

Warmwater angling was something of a folk art back then, and the grandfathers of both today's tournament bass fishermen and yuppie fly fishers were casting big bugs (made of wood, cork or hair) in murky southern rivers and catching lots of bass on the fly rod in the 1920s and 1930s, the Golden Age of warmwater fly fishing. Then, as today, the bass was considered homely and prosaic by more sophisticated angling writers and only a few (you can almost count them on the fingers of one hand) availed themselves of these fisheries. The bass has always been the fish of the common man and it remains so today. Despite the fact that there is no discernible snobbery in the writings of warmwater anglers during the Golden Age,

fly fishing somehow lost the common folks along the
way, country people that once shared an adoration of
the fly rod. Their progeny have been successfully
courted by the bass fishing colossus and have completely rejected such innocent pursuits as bass bugging, splat fishing and jiggling. Real fly fishing, with
its artistic and intellectual subtleties, will never have
mass appeal, regardless of the species of fish, but the
basic practice of fishing with the fly rod, stripped to
its bare essentials without all the arcane trappings
and adherence to tradition, was quite popular until
recent decades.

Fly fishing for largemouth bass seems to have
been born in the pristine Everglades of the Seminole
Nation. These native Americans and the runaway
Africans that they helped hide from the iron shackles
of the dreaded slaver, were using a fifteen-foot
wooden pole to poke a "bob" along the edges of a
weed-choked marsh when the naturalist, William
Bartram, traveled through Florida ten years after
Cornwallis surrendered at Yorktown in 1781. The
largemouth had been known to Europeans since at
least 1562, when the French explorer, René
Laudoniere, plucked one out of a Seminole fish trap,
but was of no interest to anglers until the publication
of Bartram's journal. Bartram described the practice of
"bobbing" with a crude fly tied on a homemade
treble hook with "white deer hair and bits of a red
garter." The "bob" was then fished on a very short
line tied to the tip of a long pole. This indigenous
form of fly fishing was practiced throughout the
eighteenth century among the Seminoles, and probably in Georgia and the Carolinas as well. I think it is
likely, considering the nature of the materials and the
obvious European influence, that the first "bob" may
have been tied and fished by one of the runaway
Africans that lived among the Seminoles. Although
the concept of fashioning a fish lure with feathers and
hair is clearly of European origin, crude forms of fly
tying were also practiced by native peoples from coast
to coast. Northeastern tribes were exposed to Anglo-
style fly fishing in the seventeenth century, and the
idea worked its way west and south as French and
English soldiers of fortune penetrated the virgin
continent. Indians of the mountain West may have

fashioned trout flies from deer, elk and caribou hair long before the explorations of Lewis and Clark.

The recorded history of *warmwater* fly fishing centers around three major figures: a New York physician who discovered it in the postbellum nineteenth century, a dry-fly purist from England who nearly destroyed it in the middle of the twentieth century and a creative fly-tier from Oklahoma who has resurrected it

## HENSHALL TO LUCAS - THE GOLDEN AGE

*"After getting the fly rod tackle ready, I thought [that] if the water gets rough, the bass bugs won't do much good . . . so I set up a bait casting outfit."*
                                    *Ray Bergman, 1942*

While Dr. James Henshall, the father of warmwater fly fishing, was the first to write about black bass, he did not discover the sport of fishing for them. Robert B. Roosevelt, Teddy's uncle and prominent angler of the day, had been casting flies to bass for some years before he formally introduced this uniquely American sport to the angling public in 1862. We can glean from his writings, along with Thaddeus Norris and others, that real warmwater fly fishing seems to have originated on the smallmouth streams of Kentucky in the 1840's. A French naturalist, Pierre Boucher, had written of the smallmouth bass two centuries earlier, and colonial fly fishers had certainly been familiar with that fish since the earliest days of settlement, but it was considered a trash fish and only taken incidentally while angling for brook trout. Henshall attributes that attitude to the fact that bass did not live in British waters and any fish, or other creature, that was native only to the New World was rough, coarse and second rate. If Henshall didn't invent sportfishing for smallmouth bass, he certainly popularized it in his classic *Book of the Black Bass*, published in 1881.

While he admired and practiced the art of fly fishing, even stating "Fly-fishing holds the same relation to bait fishing that poetry does to prose," Henshall was anything but a purist. He devotes more space to other fishing methods in his book, and would, as conditions required, troll a spoon or even resort to live bait. In fact he made a science of bait fishing, saying that "casting the minnow is quite an art, as much so as casting the fly," and would retain his affection for fishing the live minnow until his death in 1925. This versatility, a willingness to employ alternative tackle and techniques, would characterize bass fishing until the "Whitlock Revolution" in the late twentieth century.

The overwhelming majority of bass fishers used live bait exclusively in those days, but the fly rod was the tool of choice among those who preferred artificials, and remained so until the end of World War II. As yet unencumbered by the English dry-fly tradition, American bass bugging flowered after the turn of the century. Although Henshall's advocacy of bait fishing was challenged by some sophisticated anglers, they made no moral judgments about switching to the casting rod, or fly casting a small lure, whenever conditions precluded surface action. Most kept both outfits at the ready and used them with equal proficiency. Rod builders even made "convertible" fly rods that could be quickly switched to a casting rod by simply turning around the butt section.

There was neither a stigma attached to bait-casting tackle, nor had the fly rod become a symbol of social status. That kind of thinking, the rigid polarization that we see today, did not develop until the 1960s and 1970s. Traditional trout fishers of an earlier day, respected anglers like Ray Bergman and Joe Brooks, understood that fishing for the black bass demands an attitude adjustment. They made that adjustment by erecting a "philosophical wall" between trout and bass. "Although I am a trout angler and have all the dry-fly fisherman's prejudices," Bergman writes in 1942, "I forget them all when fishing for bass." Bergman would not take such liberties with bluegill, which, because of their insect eating behavoir, he philosophically grouped with the venerated trouts.

During the Golden Age of warmwater fly fishing folks could enjoy most of the creature comforts that we know today, at least those that really count, without the drawbacks of pollution, overfishing and an exploding population. When Wall Street crashed in the middle of the Golden Age, most of the waters west of the Appalachians, both warm and cold, were still pristine—sweet, pure and full of fish. Even depressions, wars and natural disasters don't stop determined anglers, who somehow always manage to find their way to the good waters, which may have been right across the street in those unspoiled times. Ray Bergman fished them all, from Lake Henshaw in Southern California to the St. John in the wild North Woods. He drifted the White River before Bull Shoals spoiled that best of smallmouth fisheries, waded the Buffalo when there was no aluminum hatch, and cast a popper to Okeechobee bass when the Everglades were still whole. Twenty-two bass rose to his bug in less than an hour on Lake Henshaw, sometime in the thirties, but I fished that same lake twenty years later and found it crowded, ruined, fished-out. I came along thirty years too late. The turn of the century was the time for a fly fisher to be born! It's sad to contemplate that our grandchildren will most certainly look back at our times with similar nostalgia. When I was an undergraduate at U.S.C. my favorite professor, a senior historian of great sagacity, proclaimed that "these are the good old days." I would unfortunately come to understand what he meant; I didn't know it then, but they were indeed. But enough sentimentality; we have to make the most of what we have left, and that's what this book is about.

The origins of the cork popper have been somewhat unclear since it first appeared nearly a century ago. Dr. Henshall knew nothing of such bugs in 1881, but Ray Bergman was fishing with one on the waters of the Hudson River valley shortly after the turn of the century. Ernest Peckinpaugh, whose famous Peck's Popper was a staple in the box of every Golden Age fly rodder, insisted that he invented the popping bug, but there is no documentary evidence to support that claim. Tom McNally would, as late as 1978, echo the prevailing view and credit Peckinpaugh with tying the prototype design. Outdoor writers of the Golden Age dance around the subject. Robert Page Lincoln, bass fisher par excellence and warmwater historian, diplomatically referred to Peckinpaugh as the "founder" of the lure, and, with similar caution, Dick Stewart would state forty years later that Peckinpaugh "introduced" the popping bug.

*The typical cork popper has changed little from its origins almost a century ago.*

Who tied the first popper? I get the feeling
from the old literature that the likes of Brooks,
Bergman and Knight knew all along who created it,
but were hesitant to flatly contradict Peckinpaugh, an
important commercial figure. They must have cringed
when John B. Thompson, better known as "Ozark
Ripley," let the cat out of the bag in his forgotten 1924
work, *Bass and Bass Fishing.* According to the outspo-
ken Thompson, the first popper was carved and
dressed in 1903 by none other than the father of the
American dry-fly, the legendary Theodore Gordon.
Thompson added that bugs similar to Gordon's tie
mysteriously appeared on the White River in 1905
and we also know that Ray Bergman discovered them
at about the same time in upstate New York.

The design was apparently unknown before
that because neither Eugene McCarthy, writing in
1900, nor William C. Harris, in his 1905 book, revealed any awareness of the popping bug. Neither
writer includes it, nor anything like it, in his discussion of known bass patterns. Harris does present,
however, two American bass patterns, both tied in the
manner of classic salmon flies, from the deep South:
the Cracker, "named after poor Georgia whites," and
the William D. Cleveland. Cleveland was a prominent
Texas businessman who, incidentally, was a member
of the mysterious Texas Fishing Club, a small,
wealthy group of split-cane purists who fished the
rivers of East Texas in the late nineteenth century
(not to be confused with President Grover Cleveland,
also an ardent bass angler).

*Most early "bass flies"
were simply large
versions of trout and
salmon wet flies.*

After carefully reading much of the
warmwater literature from that era, I am convinced
that the first popper did not come from Peckinpaugh's
vise, and I am inclined to believe Thompson, but
revising fly fishing history to reflect Gordon's contribution may be premature. I am troubled that Robert
Page Lincoln, a careful researcher who was close to
the primary sources, most of whom were still alive
when he wrote *Black Bass Fishing*, did not pick up on
the Gordon connection. It is possible, if unlikely, that
he overlooked Thompson's work, but it could also be
that he discounted it as myth. Absolute confirmation
would require a review of Gordon's voluminous
correspondence, but that's beyond the scope of this

work. In any case, Peckinpaugh's tale, about getting
the idea for the bug when a bass grabbed a cork bottle
stopper that he accidentally dropped in the river,
sounds like early Madison Avenue to me.

Turn of the century fly fisher, conservationist
and famous writer, Emerson Hough, whose best-
selling novel, *The Covered Wagon*, would later become
the prototype of all western movies, is credited with
tying the first deer-hair fly about 1912. Hough, who
traveled widely in the untamed West, insisted that he
got the idea for his pattern while in Montana, from
native Americans. Deer hair was readily available in
the world of the Crow, Blackfoot and Nez Perce, who
used it to fashion large trout flies. Based on Hough's
observations, some form of practical fly fishing was
well established among these peoples before the turn
of the century. It would seem plausible that the
concept of practical fly tying was introduced to
mountain tribes by an anonymous white trapper who
traded fish hooks for beaver pelts. If only we could
see one of those early Indian flies, but they have
likely been lost forever to antiquity. The rest of the
story would have been similarly lost had it not been
for the efforts of Minnesota angler, Robert Page
Lincoln, who carefully researched the origins of the
hair bug.

Byron Dalrymple states in his comprehensive
*Modern Book of the Black Bass*, the first deer hair "bug"
was developed not for bass, but rather for big brown
trout on Michigan streams before the First World War.
This was probably Emerson Hough's version of the
original Indian tie, since Hough fished primarily
around Sault St. Marie, but the fly was actually a very
large dry and it did not have a spun or stacked body.
Lincoln discovered that the first deer-hair bass bug, as
we know it today, was the brainchild of O.C. Tuttle of
Old Forge, New York. Tuttle's bug proved to be a
bass killer and was responsible for the popularization
of the design. The Buckhair Mouse and the Henshall
Bug, widely marketed by the Weber Life-Like Fly
Company throughout the Golden Age, were based on
Tuttle's creation, according to Lincoln.

Joe Messinger was still a young man when
Tuttle tied his bug, and had stacked hair flies well
before World War I, but he doesn't enter the official

record until he returned from war-torn France.
(Messinger introduced his wonderful little frog in
1925.) It could well be that both Messinger and Tuttle
developed the lure independently, but the official
credit must go to Tuttle. So, then, although Emerson
Hough did not tie the first bass bug, he and his
Blackfoot friends were a vital link in the process. Few
modern anglers are aware of the Indian origins of
deer-hair fly tying, although Dick Stewart acknowledges it in his introduction to *Flies for Bass and
Panfish*. I knew that the story was hidden somewhere
in trout lore, but I thought the answer lay buried in a
Catskill valley, certainly not on the wild rivers of the
frontier West. Most significant warmwater tying
techniques have, in fact, come from trout tiers. Even
the leech type rabbit-strip flies that we depend on so
heavily today was introduced to American trout
fishers through Dan Byford's Zonker pattern. (Rabbit
fur strips had already been used on flies by New
Zealand fishermen.)

Messinger originated many more deer-hair
patterns after his pioneering frog. Although he may
not have invented the technique, he certainly refined
it. His unique method of lashing the hair to the shank
with half-hitches produced a much more durable and
more tightly packed body than modern spinning
methods. Tuttle and his contemporaries may have
tied with alternating bands of color, but the lateral
separation of colors (white belly/colored back) was
original with Messinger. He, and to a lesser extent
Ray Bergman, sought to imitate actual warmwater
organisms. Messinger spent riverside evenings tying
flies in the back seat of his old sedan, along with
collecting, identifying, and sketching the aquatic and
terrestrial insects that gathered around the dome
light. He carried live chickens in a special pen in the
open trunk of the vintage Hudson, and plucked them
as he needed hackle. When a rooster had given his all,
it was summarily butchered and eaten. The old
adage, "waste not, want not," was necessarily gospel
in depression-era Appalachia. Messinger was not a
physician, attorney or wealthy businessman playing at
fly fishing. He was a self-educated, Appalachian coal
miner who supplemented his modest veteran's
pension by tying bass bugs and trout flies. He didn't

*A Messinger frog.*

write much, but he was a very intelligent, talented and highly respected fly fisher ("superb" is the word Lincoln uses to describe him) who regularly fished with the most famous anglers of his day, including his friend, John Alden Knight.

Knight was a popular fishing writer who extolled the pleasures of fly fishing for bass in many articles and books and, as we saw in the preceding chapter, he developed the solunar tables. Again, the fly rod was always presented as the tool of choice whenever bass were surface oriented, but there is not a hint of purism or snobbery in the writings of any of these warmwater fly fishing progenitors. On the contrary, most of them carried bait casting gear at all times and used it regularly and unabashedly. Joe Messinger was an exception. He used the fly rod exclusively but, as his son adamantly emphasizes, he had no "purist" philosophy and did not look down his nose at friends, Ray Bergman and Jack Knight, when they fished with bait casting gear. When there was no topwater action, Joe was satisfied to put a spinner blade in front of the fly and let it sink. He was, however, much impressed with the spinning reel when it was invented after World War II and promptly bought one, but it never replaced his beloved fly rod. Joe Messinger, Sr., always the humble man, passed away in 1966 after seventy-four wonderful, bass-filled years, and would doubtless be embarrassed that we have given him so much attention.

Anglers of the Golden Age restricted their use of the fly rod to the top few feet of the water column although Ray Bergman and a young Ted Trueblood, who would later become editor of *Field & Stream*, continued to use the classic wet flies that Dr. Henshall had discussed a half century earlier (old patterns like Parmacheene Belle and Black Palmer, tied on sizes two and four snelled hooks). Bergman often fished a pair of wet flies on a dropper rig, and retrieved them very fast, sometimes even skidding them across the surface. Dr. Henshall seems to have gone entirely over to bait fishing in his later years and shows a definite preference for the minnow in his last book, *Bass, Pike, Perch* published six years before he passed away at the age of eighty-nine.

While those fellows also enjoyed nature

*Old wet flies like this Parmacheene Belle were usually snelled.*

during their jaunts afield, and often waxed poetic on
the magnificence of the Creation, warmwater fly
fishing had not yet become so ethereal and cerebral
that the common man could no longer identify with
it. The decline, even "death" might not be too strong
a word, of bass bugging after World War II is due to a
number of factors. It seems ironic that the demise of
bass bugging as a popular sport was presided over by
an angler who learned fly fishing on the hallowed
brown trout waters of England. The decline of bass
bugging after the war is attributable to the introduction of the spinning reel, the building of the big
impoundments, affordable bass boats and tournament
fishing. But that movement also had its guru. The
father of modern bass fishing, the idol of the rapidly
growing ranks of competition-oriented bass men, was
an English-born dry-fly purist by the name of Jason
Lucas, who had cut his angling teeth on Halford
and Skues.

## LUCAS TO WHITLOCK - THE DARK AGE

*"Bass bugging is an extremely crude form of fly fishing, if fly
fishing it can be called . . . A child of average mentality
should learn bass bugging in a few minutes."*
　　　　　　　　　　　　　　　　　　*Jason Lucas, 1947*

*"Fly rod fishing for bass, and particularly bass-bug fishing,
is the most difficult form of freshwater angling."*
　　　　　　　　　　　　　　　　　　*Jack Knight, 1949*

　　It is impossible for a modern fly fisher to
return to 1947 for an evening with the original edition
of *Lucas on Bass Fishing* without getting angry. His
flippant, almost smart-aleck tone is infuriating. The
contrasting views in the above quotes mark the
beginning of the still deepening schism between bass
fishing and fly fishing. Lucas prevailed in that debate
because, as painful as it is to admit, he was right, at
least from a pragmatic point of view. The fly rod was
no longer the most efficient tool for bass and it would
never be again. Lucas put America's most popular
gamefish forever in the domain of the casting rod,
and, to be perfectly honest, that may be where it
belongs. It is very important to emphasize, however,

that Lucas, also an ardent dry-fly trout fisher, was one
of the first to recognize the fly fishing value of the
smaller sunfish. He placed bluegill and other insect-
feeding bream on a par with trout, and considered the
fly rod the very best tool for their capture. Lucas had
impeccable fly fishing credentials and that's why it
hurts so much to read his writings on bass. He did
acknowledge that bass bugging is fun, although crude
and inefficient, and, to his credit, he encouraged all
bass fishers to become proficient with the fly rod
(advice that seems to have been forgotten). Like
Bergman and Brooks before him, Lucas does not carry
his trout baggage to the bass lake. Reading *Lucas on
Bass Fishing* reinforced my own philosophical wall
between trout and stillwater bass. Trout, along with
the lesser sunfish, are vulnerable to "real" fly fishing
all of the time, but the latter are "catchable" on a fly
only occasionally.

I grew up in western trout country and,
although I have talked with a few elderly "splat"
fishers since moving to Texas, I was acquainted with
only one real "bass bugger" back when this activity
was still vogue. But I did not consider him a fly fisher
in the usual sense of the term. So, with that hindsight,
I grudgingly understand Lucas's criticism of bass
bugging. Back in the late 50s and early 60s I started
each season, before the Sierras thawed out, casting
dry flies to small bluegills on Snodgrass Slough in the
Sacramento Delta. I didn't take it very seriously, but
it was a fun way to limber up the arm for the coming
summer of trout fishing. I often shared this water with
Ranch Lee, a bug-fishing throwback to the Golden
Age, who fished the slough every evening when he
finished work at a Ford dealership in the nearby
village of Galt. He was a friendly, outgoing sort of
person, as car salesmen are inclined to be, who
actually sold me a new 1960 Falcon while in the act of
playing a three-pound bass. He always had several
nice fish on the stringer when I arrived, but I didn't
have any equipment that would cast his bugs and I
wasn't interested in obtaining any. I was satisfied with
the bluegills that I took on my trout flies. I did,
however, enjoy watching Ranch use a stiff glass fly
rod, equipped with an automatic reel and level line,
to cast a big cork popper on a short, heavy leader. As

Lucas said, this was an extremely crude form of fly
fishing. Ranch was a fairly young man and, instead of
continuing as a fly fisher, there is little doubt in my
mind that he eventually bought a bass boat and a
casting rod and joined the new tournament craze that
was well underway at that time. The saddest form of
historical analysis is to speculate on "what might have
been," and it's such a pity that Lucas chose to lead
thousands of anglers away from the fly rod and into
modern bass fishing instead of helping them become
real fly fishers.

I had forgotten all about Ranch Lee and bass
bugging when I bought a little piece of Texas in 1979.
The real-estate salesman considered himself a fellow
fly fisher and invited me to go fishing with him. I
naturally jumped at the chance to visit prime local
waters, but discovered that he was not a fly fisher in
my California understanding of the term. He was a
classical bass bugger whose tackle and techniques
were identical to Ranch's some twenty years before.
He explained that nearly all the anglers in his rural
area had bought big boats and now fished the impoundments with casting rods, but that he and a very
few others elected to stay with the old ways. He
outfished me badly that day—very badly!

My trout gear and angling style just didn't cut
the mustard on Texas bass. When I complained about
my poor performance to a local old timer, he sized it
up: "Shooot," he drawled, "Bud ain't no fly fisherman, he just splaaat fishes." I would come to understand, in due course, what the old boy meant. While
Bud and I have become good friends over the years,
and have shared a number of business deals, our
fishing relationship never developed. Still, it's
refreshing that a few have resisted the tournament
attitude of modern bass fishing.

Maybe it's unfair to blame the whole tournament thing on Jason Lucas, but the spirit of competition runs throughout his writings. He achieved his
greatest fame when he fished for eight hours a day for
365 consecutive days in order to prove, I guess, that
he was the greatest angler of all time. People were
impressed with his unique brand of angling showmanship. He presented his "Dirty Tricks Department," where he taught the fledgling bass fisher to

keep his spots secret and how to find the other fellow's spots. He gets angry at other anglers and clearly enjoys showing them up. He hides his good fish by "kicking them under the stern seat" when another boat approaches, and is inclined to ridicule those who lack his skills. While "mean-spirited" may be too strong, and perhaps this was simply a natural reaction to the increasing number of anglers on public waters after the war, I still see in Lucas the seeds of arrogance that sadly characterizes so many "bass pros" and amateur tournament fishermen today. Moreover, he knows what he's doing, even prefacing his dirty tricks by admonishing the reader that ". . . if your conscience is tender don't read the rest of this chapter . . ." There is nothing like this in the writings of his predecessors, nor, for that matter, anywhere else in the history of angling. He must have struck a chord among rank and file bass anglers, though, because he was immensely popular. Still, his approach (at least during his early years) was "ugly" as we say in Texas, and I don't like it.

Lucas mellowed with age, and his rhetoric moderated. In the 1962 edition of his book, he assumes a more conciliatory posture and even avocates bass bugging. It was too late though, the casting rod had already won and fewer warmwater fly rodders remained.

*Bass Bug Fishing*, by Joe Brooks also appeared in 1947. His traditional, gentlemanly, quiet presentation of warmwater angling is in sharp contrast to Lucas's strident tone, and seems to have been lost in the furor over the emerging casting rod. That year seems to mark the beginning of the Dark Ages of warmwater fly fishing and Ray Bergman would lament that there was a "growing apathy toward fly fishing on the part of bass anglers." Bergman could see, along with his contemporaries from the Golden Age, that the sport was dying; that his beloved fly rod was rapidly disappearing from warmwaters. In 1938, Wallace Gallagher lamented that fly rodders had shrunk to a minority of one in ten on bass waters (today it's more like one in a thousand).

The organization of the first bass club was in 1938, while Joe Brooks and others formed The Brotherhood of the Jungle Cock just before the War.

The respective credos of these seminal organizations removed all doubt that bass fishers and fly fishers would no longer share the same philosophical bed. Lucas, who was the fishing editor of *Sports Afield* for many years, rejoiced in that estrangement with characteristic animosity:

". . . I stick up for the casting rod because it has been the underdog. But every dog will turn, and when the casting rod does, I hope it bites some of the smug fly rod men where it hurts most . . . I'll settle for some treble hooks through the seats of pants . . ."

(Maybe "mean-spirited" isn't too strong, after all.)

Warmwater fly fishing languished for two decades until Dave Whitlock breathed some life back into it. A survey of the literature during the 50s and 60s reveals only an occasional article on panfishing or old style bass bugging. There were no significant fly fishing developments in those decades, as bass buggers fled *en masse* to the casting rod and coldwater fly fishers bade them good riddance. But there was a new dawn breaking as trout fishers began, very slowly and reluctantly, to explore other species of fish. The Federation of Fly Fishers (F.F.F.) was founded in 1966, on the principle that all gamefish are worthy of our attention and respect. I won't forget the bitter debate in my California club at the time over whether we should join this upstart organization that believed saltwater and warmwater fish were, God forbid, suitable prey for the fly rod. The F.F.F. advocates barely carried the day and some disgruntled members even dropped out of the club, preferring to stay with Trout Unlimited. The trout continued to reign supreme, however, and still does today, even, in new clubs that are forming here in the Deep South. Although I try to encourage more anglers to give sunfish a chance, especially in these hard-pressed times, I have accepted the reality that bass and other sunfish will be only salmonoid surrogates through my lifetime. But, to paraphrase Lucas, "every dog has its day."

Wisconsin angler, Sid Gordon, represented the new breed of fly fisher that was emerging. Gordon acknowledges in his little heralded but excellent 1955 work, *How to Fish From Top to Bottom*, that other fresh

water species—bass, muskellunge, walleye—also
have fly fishing potential. He doesn't address saltwater fish, probably because of his geographical location
in the midwest. Gordon approaches these surrogate
fishes without modifying his coldwater orientation
one wit. I regret that I hadn't read his book when I
wrote *The Sunfishes*, because he is expressing the same
sentiments that have guided my warmwater career, at
least as far as bream are concerned.

Unlike fly fishers of the Golden Age, Gordon
erects no wall between cold and warmwaters. While
he fully understands the habits and diet of the largemouth black bass, and knows that his dry-fly techniques will take only a few small fish, he doesn't give
a damn. He would not have disagreed with Lucas's
factual conclusions but (and this is the key to his
approach) he is always first and foremost the trout
fisher wherever he fishes and whatever species he
seeks. He would rather imitate the crane fly he
observed "dipping" into the water ("as high as
twenty-three such dips," he said) with typical
coldwater precision. He fished for bass not with a
bug, but with the dry fly and enjoyed it immensely,
although his heart, unlike the bass buggers of an
earlier era, was always on the trout stream.

The wall that Bergman had erected between
trout and bass was crumbling as fly fishers increasingly adopted Gordon's view. A keen student of
nature, as real fly fishers are inclined to be, Gordon
carried his skills of observation to the bass lake and
once observed a school of bluegills attacking a "ball"
of catfish fry. This is a phenomenon that I have seen
many times but is, along with most other warmwater
feeding events, generally ignored by trout fishers
when they visit these waters. Sid Gordon and the
newly gentrified fly fishers that he represents were
beginning to acknowledge the value of the lesser
sunfish as fly rod prey. Ernest Schwiebert's monu-
mental best seller, *Matching the Hatch*, also published
in 1955, undoubtedly stole some of the fly fisherman's
attention from Gordon's work.

One southern bass-bug fisherman who re-
fused to abandon the fly rod was Tom Nixon of Lake
Charles, Louisiana. Tom was neither part of the
Whitlock Revolution nor the new breed of genteel

warmwater anglers represented by Sid Gordon. His
*Fly Tying and Fly Fishing for Bass and Panfish*, published in 1968 (revised in 1977), offered a fly fishing
alternative to the casting rod. Nixon presented a sort
of middle way, that was based on practical realities,
considerable personal experience, and a deep understanding of the bass and its habits. For a variety of
reasons the bulk of the fly fishing community has not
listened to him. I believe that had we not bypassed
Nixon, who offered an intermediate step in our
evolution, the exodus to the casting rod would not
have been so dramatic and final. Instead, the fly
fishing community prematurely embraced idealistic
concepts whose time had not yet come. We are going
to look carefully at Nixon's work in Chapter Five.
The sport is still languishing and desperately needs
an infusion of the Nixon's kind of pragmatism.

Tom McNally was a contemporary of Nixon
and expressed similar views. His *Fly Fishing* was
published ten years after Nixon's work and it received
the same cool response from the new breed of well-
heeled professionals that now dominate the sport.
Sculpted deer hair and tanned rabbit hide became the
rage. The rubber-leg poppers, pork rind strips and
spinner blades that McNally and Nixon talked about
were embarrassingly locked in the closet.
Neither man is given adequate
recognition in today's fly
fishing community.
The standard cork
bug that most of us
cut our warmwater
teeth on—slanted
face and tapered body,
dressed sparsely with
splayed feather tails and
single hackle skirt—was originated by
Tom McNally and further popularized by his son,
Bob, another talented warmwater angler who also got
lost in the purism of the 1980s.

*McNally frog*

There were barely enough Nixons and
McNallys around during those dark years to keep the
old sport alive, and the new generation would never
embrace the black bass as the old timers once had. A
renaissance of warmwater fishing would have to wait

for a couple of decades until a talented gentleman from Oklahoma came along.

Dave Whitlock spoke directly to those fly fishers who were willing to try different fisheries, but the ensuing "revolution" brought neither large numbers of fly fishers to warmwaters nor did it have any impact at all on the bassing world. He spoke to an enthusiastic, but disappointingly small, group of anglers. His new artistic approach was infinitely more sophisticated than the earlier bass bugging. Despite a plethora of publicity, and the fact that his trouting credentials commanded the respect and attentive ear of knowledgeable fly fishers, Dave had trouble selling warmwater species to the new, upscale fly fisher. Conversely, the Whitlock philosophy was far too aesthetic, impractical and idealistic for the now well-developed bass fishing culture that Jason Lucas created thirty years earlier. Dave, and those of us who followed him, were quite literally "betwixt and between." I have heard him express disappointment that the bass people wouldn't listen. As he often says, "fly fishing has so much to offer them." Dave has tried to encourage a reconciliation, unlike another famous fly fisher who once told me, when I suggested that we try to establish some sort of dialog with the tournament world, that he wanted "no part of the bastards." Although he advocates very different alternatives, Whitlock acknowledges the potential of Tom Nixon's middle way and included Nixon's newly revised book as an important fly tying reference in a 1978 article he wrote for *Outdoor Life*. The late 1970s was a time, like the late 40s, of great change and decision. The conservative Nixon offered a slower, evolutionary approach, while the more idealistic Whitlock represented an appealing departure from the mainstream of the bass bugging past. I, along with most of my fly fishing brethren, joined the latter school, which still prevails today.

## THE WHITLOCK REVOLUTION
*"I am not a purist. If live bait were the best way to catch bass, I'd probably fish bait exclusively."*
*John Alden Knight, 1949*

It is inconceivable that any modern fly fisher would

make such an extraordinary statement. We have gone
from such extreme pragmatism to an equally extreme
kind of quixotic idealism. When Lucas redefined the
mainstream, warmwater fly fishing was thereby
cleansed of all such impurities as it gained acceptance
among a new breed of "politically-correct" anglers
during the late 1960s and 70s. Taboos were applied to
alternative tackle and the schism between the fly
fishing and bass fishing worlds that started with Lucas
widened to the point of total mutual exclusion—
neither side spoke to the other anymore! Before Ray
Scott founded Bass Anglers Sportsmans Society
(B.A.S.S.) in 1968, any book on bass fishing that did
not include at least a chapter on fly fishing would
have been unthinkable. But things changed. Bass
fishing personality John Weiss could write a detailed
treatise on the subject in 1976 without even mention-
ing the fly rod. Fly fishing was changing too. It was no
longer simply a fun way to catch bass when conditions
were right. It had become a statement of social caste,
a way of life, a means of defining oneself philosophically, socially and economically.

    Dave Whitlock is closely
associated with these fly-fishing
developments because he
brought dignity, artistry
and class to bass
bugging—that
was just what
we wanted. He
was the first famous
bass bugger (there's g
ot to be a better term)
in history who did not,
with the lone exception
of Messinger, occasionally
use the casting rod. There
was a time when I would have
been absolutely devastated to think about Dave
Whitlock even touching a plastic worm. As I have
come to understand the black bass, I will now be
disappointed if he doesn't give them a try.

*A Most-Whit
Hairbug.*

    In the 1970s there seemed to be a small
resurgence of interest in bass bugging. In *Outdoor Life*
(March 1978), Dave, with characteristic humility,

attributed this to the Gaddabout Gaddis TV show, and he quoted Lee Wulff, who said that Gaddis "opened the closet and let the bug fly out." While the hoped for renaissance never really developed, at least not among rank and file fly fishers, Dave gave warmwater angling renewed respectability in what had come to be perceived as an elitist fly fishing community. In the tradition of Joe Messinger, whose Hair Frog represented an early acknowledgement of actual warmwater food forms, Dave made bass bugging respectable. Solid coldwater credentials and exceptional fly-tying skills gave him credibility with this new breed of well-educated, affluent, sometimes "yuppie" fly fishers, and his warmwater advocacy received a degree of approbation that had been denied to many of his predecessors. The application of trouting approaches and philosophy to warmwater, which is the real essence of Dave's contribution, is eminently appropriate for smaller, insect-feeding sunfish but, I hope he will agree, it must be tempered with pragmatism in the pursuit of Mr. Bigmouth.

Every religion has to spread the word in order to thrive, but there was no magazine devoted exclusively to fly fishing until 1969 when Don Zahner founded *Fly Fisherman*. The appearance of that publication, along with the organization of the Federation of Fly Fishers, fueled what I like to call the Whitlock Revolution. *Fly Fisherman* gave voice to the narrower, purist views of fly fishing that were beginning to emerge. Before there were fly-fishing periodicals and organizations, bass bugging and panfishing were necessarily confined within popular parameters. The blossoming of these specialized publications encouraged warmwater fly fishers to join the trout fly fisher in a self-imposed exile from the rest of the angling community, a trend that continues today. It is this very isolation that is responsible for the prevailing upscale image of fly fishing. Whitlock tried on many occasions to deter this trend, to keep warmwater fly fishing alive as a popular sport, but even from his position as the most influential figure in the field, he could not alter the march of history and we lost the average angler, the everyday working man who once preferred the fly rod.

Other fly-fishing periodicals soon blossomed,

providing further impetus for the Whitlock Revolution. Dave's innovative fly designs, which he presented in historic articles in *Sports Afield, Outdoor Life,* and *Fly Tyer* in the late 1970s, changed the sport forever. In addition to colorful topwater bugs, warmwater fly fishers now were being offered subsurface alternatives to casting and spinning lures, and these flies were even commanding a growing interest and respect from coldwater fly fishermen.

Prior to the introduction of these creative subsurface flies from Dave Whitlock and his followers, fly rodders used various kinds of hardware with impunity. Tackle manufacturers once offered scaled-down versions of popular lures that were light enough to fish on the old enameled GBF lines. In fact, the fly rod was the only way to fish very small lures before the spinning reel appeared in the late 1940s. Ray Bergman complained that he disliked the "crippled casts and clumsy retrieves" that came with attempting to fly cast a lure. It was common and accepted practice to cast—or at least chuck, sling, lop, dap or heave—a small Flatfish, Dardevle or Johnson Spoon on a fly line, and the practice wasn't restricted to warmwater. Fly rod lures for trout were sold by many suppliers. I used to cast a small Flatfish to big brookies in high-country lakes thirty years ago, and the practice was widely accepted by all but the snobbiest of dry-fly purists. Was it fly fishing? Any answer to that must be subjective and is a matter of semantics; I certainly don't hesitate to call it "fly rodding." These days I spend a lot of time "bassin' with a fly rod."

*Dardevle*

In any case, the art of fishing a lure on the fly rod was lost as a different philosophy took over. I think this skill must be resurrected if the fly rod is ever to be a viable alternative to the casting rod. With today's improved equipment, it is a lot easier than in Bergman's day. My experience and experiments have led me to conclude that the realities of bass behavior demand some backtracking and a return to the use of fly rod lures under certain conditions. A fly rodder's orientation is, and should be, vastly different from the tournament bass fisher's, and I am not suggesting a Bill Dance or Jimmy Houston approach to bass fishing. My premise is simply to allow our credo to crack just enough to allow the use of lures for deep, lethargic bass. Wallace Gallagher, a highly respected fly fisher from the Golden Age, put it best: "There are a few anglers of the present day who pretend to be shocked at the idea of using any other than the artificial fly as a lure cast for the fly rod. This is foolish. Any lure is legitimate that admits of sportsmanlike use with suitable tackle."

Indeed, some modern warmwater experts—Lefty Kreh and Larry Dahlberg come immediately to mind—still switch back and forth with impunity. But, they wear two hats and Lefty rarely mentions that he is a world class spin fisher to a flyfishing audience. Those who carried the torch between Henshall and Lucas would not hesitate to discuss both tools, but we have a tendency to venerate only those aspects of the Golden Age that don't seem to clash with our contemporary ideology. Bergman, Messinger, Brooks, Knight and the countless thousands of fly rod anglers that emulated them deserve more respect than that.

1562
René Laudoniere discovers largemouth bass while exploring Florida
1664
Pierre Boucher writes about smallmouth bass
1791
William Bartram describes "bobbing" for bass
Seminole Nation - African Americans
1862
Robert B. Roosevelt introduces bass fishing as a sport
1881
Dr. James Henshall- the father of bass fishing
William Harris

1903
Bass bugging born

| | | |
|---|---|---|
| Crow Nation | | |
| Emerson Hough | | |
| | | |
| O.C. Tuttle | The Golden Age | |
| | | |
| 1925 | Ozark Ripley | |
| Joe Messinger | John Alden Knight | |
| | Wallace Gallagher | |
| | Joe Brooks | |
| | Ray Bergman | |
| | Robert Page Lincoln | |
| | | |
| The Dark Years | Victory in Europe | Spinning reels |
| | | Better casting reels |
| | A. J. McClane | |
| Sid Gordon | Ted Trueblood | 1947 |
| | B. Dalrymple | Jason Lucas |
| | | Bill Dance |
| | | |
| 1966 | 1968 | 1968 |
| FFF formed | Tom Nixon | B.A.S.S. formed |
| Charles Waterman | A.D. Livingston | |
| Dave Whitlock | Tom McNally | |
| Jimmy Nix | Larry Dahlberg | |

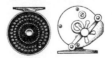

FIVE


# NONE DARE CALL IT
# FLY FISHING

*"Many times over the past years bass would refuse my
surface offerings and I would be at a decided disadvantage.
. . . At the height of my frustrations others were winching far
better than average fish up from the depths and their
comments were far from soothing."*

*Tom Nixon, 1977*

Everything is perfect for late spring bass fishing—the
weather, the late season, the small weekday crowd at
the launching ramp. You got out of bed at 3 A.M. to arrive
at first light, and you fully expect an immediate strike
when you cast the big hair bug into the shoreline brush.
Nothing doing. You fish for an hour and cover a quarter
mile of bank, but no takers. You try every topwater fly in
your box without success. What's wrong?

It's quite likely you are fishing in the wrong
place. There are no bass along the bank. They are
suspended over structure at greater depths, and you
can see a bass fisherman out there in twelve or fifteen
feet of water, chunking a worm into a submerged
hydrilla bed. He knows that the shallows are barren in
this post-spawn period and he won't fish the bank at
all until later in the fall. He's out there catching fish
and having fun while you cast to empty water. I know
how you feel at this point because I have experienced
the same emotions—dejection, a longing for friendlier
waters, a sense of isolation in an alien environment.

What are your options? You can break out the
casting rod and fish with that, which is boring. You can
stubbornly cast the bug to empty water all day, which is
silly. You can try to fly fish with a full sinking line, which
is more work than fun. You can tie a weighted fly on
your floating line, which is more viable than any of the
above, or you can give up and go home like I did for years.

## THE PROBLEM
*"There are bug days and plug days, you see."*
                                    *Ray Bergman, 1947*

I presented a fly-tying seminar to a club in Texas
some time back. I spent the morning discussing
warmwater entomology and the application of traditional trouting techniques and philosophy to angling
for bream and other sunfish. In the afternoon we
talked about bass fishing on the big Texas impoundments and I indicated that the conventional casting
rod is a vital tool there, and that the angler who fails
to use it is unnecessarily handicapping himself. Some
of the participants were understandably dumbfounded that I could contradict myself in such a
blatant way. They couldn't conceive of anyone being
such a purist while bream fishing and then resorting
to the ultimate heresy when bass fishing. I hate to
bring Jason Lucas to my defense, but when similarly
challenged he responded that "consistency is the hob
goblin of small minds."

The explanation for this apparent inconsistency lies in the fact that while traditional coldwater
approaches are as applicable to the farm pond as to
the trout stream, bass fishing in big lakes requires an
attitude adjustment, at least if you want to catch fish.
A small warmwater pond and the trout stream are
more alike than different; often combined in the same
fishery on rivers such as the New England ponds
where my friend, Steve Tofani, fishes. Trout, of
course, feed more consistently and regularly than
warmwater fish, and even sluggish bluegill can be
taken with a deep nymph, but lethargic, subsurface
largemouth are not vulnerable to any traditional fly
fishing method. In order to successfully address this
species, the fly fisher must take a lesson from
Bergman, Brooks, Whitlock and, yes, even Lucas. As
Dave Whitlock wrote a few years ago,

"Traditional trout and salmon fly fishing was
almost entirely different from what was
required to catch bass on flies. No wonder so
many fly fishers and lure casters felt the fly
rod was not equal to the job of catching
big bass!"

You may be getting weary of hearing about that

philosophical wall between trout and bass, but the very essence of this book is to redraw that dichotomy. I apologize for the redundancy, but this concept must be firmly in place before we cross that metaphorical barrier in the following discussion.

Unfortunately, stillwater largemouth only feed occasionally and I finally understand why efforts to convert bass fishers to the fly rod have failed. They have been asked to do something that doesn't work. They go fishing to have fun, not to frustrate themselves. And, they're not interested in investing years of effort to confirm some idealogical concept of "fly fishing." The crumbling of Bergman's wall, which distinguished between fishing methods, accelerated during the "Whitlock Revolution," and resulted in the alienation of the fly fishing mainstream from bass fishing. Real card-carrying, fly-tying, vest-wearing, jet-setting fly fishers could not easily adjust to warmwater, and they refused to adopt the most abundant and popular gamefish in America. This was especially true throughout largemouth bass territory. The time has come to intellectually rebuild Bergman's wall and, in his words, restore "realms of piscatorial pleasure hitherto undreamed."

Ray Bergman said that a bass would rise from a depth of eight feet to take a bug; Tom McNally extended that to twelve feet; Tom Nixon reduced it to five, and it's my opinion that "real" fly fishing for largemouth bass (as defined in the first chapter) is, realistically, restricted to the top couple of feet of the water column. It works very well when fish are actively feeding in that zone, or when conditions are such that they will opportunistically grab something that is swimming on or very near the surface. Unfortunately, as we have seen, topwater offerings are effective only at certain times of the day, in certain seasons, and under certain weather conditions. The bass-fishing literature includes scientific theories and explanations of this behavior, and even a cursory examination of those writings leads to the same conclusion: trying to catch deep bass on flies is extremely inefficient at best and a foolish exercise in futility at worst.

Bass, especially larger fish, often key on something that crawls along the bottom. On southern lakes, the bottom may be only 12 or 15 feet down. Although presenting a fly at that depth is logistically possible with a full-sinking line, and there are a few very patient, highly-skilled anglers who successfully do so, that kind of fly fishing takes more patience than I have and I find it more work than fun. It's boring, non-productive and simply not enjoyable. When I wrote *The Sunfishes*, I was still struggling to master sinking-line techniques. By now I have given up heavy sinking lines and found other alternatives. While I hope I can keep an open mind on the subject, they are no longer part of my angling repertoire.

I started the 1991 fishing season with big plans. I was going to discipline myself to fish with weighted flies, high-density lines and other subsurface techniques. It became apparent that the fly rod could never be a viable alternative to the casting rod unless ways were found to effectively fish on or near the bottom. I acquired an inventory of sinking lines, tied a lot of flies and started the season with the greatest enthusiasm. I was going to master subsurface techniques, write a blockbuster article and put together a dynamite slide show on deep water bassin'.

Well, so much for "the best-laid plans of mice and men . . ." I ended the season with more problems than solutions. Casting and handling the heavy lines and weighted flies reminded me of fishing for steelhead with homemade shooting heads in northern California during my youth. This kind of fishing was often more drudgery than sport, but at least when steelheading the current helped roll the fly along the clean freestone bottom. Strike detection and hook setting were not problems then, because the fish hooked itself on the swing.

On the positive side, my flies were as attractive to the bass as a plastic worm or any other lure, and using Uniform Sinking Lines from Scientific Anglers, I was able to present the fly right on the bottom. The problem was neither pattern nor presentation, it was strike detection. The lack of feel and sensitivity, debris gathering on the fly and, most of all, an inability to strike the fish and set the hook presented serious problems. It is conceivable that with great patience, practice and experience the strike-detection problem may ultimately be solved but, although I accidentally hooked an occasional fish, I never did learn to set up on the bass with a heavy sinking line. My efforts were often more comical than effective.

Most of this bottom fishing was done in 10 to 20 feet of heavily-vegetated water, using a variety of large rabbit-strip and saddle-hackle patterns. As Dave Whitlock says, you must maintain a straight line to the fly and strike with the line hand and rod butt. If I cast the sinking line a comfortable distance (somewhere around 60 feet or so) in 15 feet of water, the retrieve began with a substantial angle between the rod and the line. Half way through the retrieve the rod was well under the water, perhaps 45 degrees to the surface, in order to maintain a straight line. In the final 20 feet, where most strikes occurred (at least where those that I could *feel* occurred), the fly line was virtually perpendicular to the surface and striking with my stripping hand was impossible. I felt very much the fool, repeatedly jerking on the fly rod tip in a futile attempt to set the hook (visualize Oliver Hardy standing in a boat with a fly rod in his hand, trying to hook a bass, while Stan Laurel offers advice and assistance). And, this problem is only exaggerated when fishing from a float tube.

*It is impossible to sink the hook using the fly rod tip.*

I used an 8'9", 10-weight boron composite rod. It was very stiff but the tip still wasn't stout enough to drive a hook into a bass's hard jaw. I suspect that at least some of the time, the fish grabbed the rabbit-strip tail so the hook was never in its mouth. To make matters worse, the damn bass invariably swims toward you.

I did amuse my worm-chunking friends. One fishing companion laughed so hard at my efforts to hook a bass with the tip of the fly rod that he nearly fell overboard. He was lucky we were in his boat. Otherwise I would have started the motor and left him in the middle of Lake Sam Rayburn without a life jacket!

Fly fishers are in short supply in my rural area and I often find myself in the company of "heave 'n' crank" bass fishers. Day after day, year after year, I have endured these fellows taking bass consistently on soft plastic imitations of eels, salamanders and crawfish, spinner baits and various jigs while I get little action with my sinking lines and flies. I would have gladly signed a contract with the devil himself to outfish any one of them just once. Ted Trueblood wrote, many years ago, about being badly outfished by several companions who were fishing plastic worms on casting rods in a southern impoundment. Determined to make a credible showing on this "deep day," Trueblood resorted to a lead-core shooting head and a buoyant fly. By using a very fast retrieve, "foot long pulls and short pauses," he managed to detect the strikes and hook a few fish. The bass were probably actively feeding on the bottom if they responded to a fast retrieve, and remember that back when these reservoirs were new there were comparatively few anglers and unbelievable numbers of completely wild bass. Anyone who remembers casting those old shooting heads, which consisted of about twenty feet of lead-core trolling line, will realize just how desperate Trueblood must have been! I used lead-core heads for steelhead on the Klamath River back in the sixties and still have the knots on the back of my noggin to prove it.

So, although I caught an occasional fish with the various systems and assorted flies that I tried, I never really enjoyed bass fishing with sinking lines.

The rewards just didn't justify the effort. I suffered constant frustration and discouragement. There were insurmountable obstacles with strike detection, setting the hook, weeds hanging on the fly and the misery of trying to pick up a heavy, submerged line from the float tube. It just wasn't fun.

*Angler can't detect the strike
because his sinking fly line is
in heavy weeds.*

## THE SOLUTIONS

*". . . the best known way to expand any area of angling
endeavor is to whet a few appetites with something a bit out
of the ordinary . . . "*

Tom Nixon, 1977

The big breakthrough came during the winter when I decided to again read Tom Nixon's out-of-print book, *Fly Tying and Fly Fishing for Bass and Panfish*, this time with an open mind born of desperation. The answers to my problems had been there all along, right on my own bookshelf. My first introduction to Tom was on the pages of the old *Fly Tyer* magazine, to which he contributed until it evolved into today's *American Angler*. He never rang my bell, though. My trout-fishing orientation precluded ever accepting the idea of using lures on the fly rod. Tom didn't speak my language and I didn't listen to him. It now appears that the time has come for me to learn his language, which is pure Dixie bassin'.

    Although he grew up in Illinois, Tom spent much of his working life in Lake Charles, Louisiana and his fly-rod bass systems were developed on my home waters—the rivers and lakes of southeast Texas and southwest Louisiana. Since he doesn't carry trout baggage, Tom was free to address these fisheries pragmatically without the self-limiting, philosophical encumbrances that plague many other fly fishers.

I first met Tom at a conclave in Mountain Home, Arkansas. I attended his seminar on warmwater angling, but he lost me when he said to cut a foot off the tip of the fly rod in order to cast heavy spinner baits dressed with surveyor's tape. That seminar consisted of mostly coldwater anglers and Tom's hybridizing of conventional bass fishing and fly fishing went too far afield for most of us to accept at the time. The highlight of the afternoon came when Tom related an incident that occurred some years earlier while he was fishing a Louisiana bayou. It seems that Tom drew glances from two Cajuns in a nearby boat when he released a couple of small bass. The polite glances turned to icy stares when he released a two pounder. A few minutes later, Tom released a beautiful fish that would top four pounds. "What's it gonna take," one of the Cajuns inquired of his companion, "to satisfy that fella?"

I also met Ron Knight at the same conclave. Ron is a dedicated disciple of Tom Nixon and he has tried to explain to me for years that I must put aside my trout-fishing frame of mind to consistently catch bass in big, southern waters. I resisted his views but now realize that he was right all along. Ron is able to shift philosophical gears when he moves from insect feeding trout and sunfish to subsurface bass. Coldwater tackle, approaches and techniques work efficiently on the former, but they are woefully ineffective for the latter. I have learned from Tom Nixon that although you cannot always fly fish for bass, you can usually bass fish with the fly rod. It is important to make this distinction to appreciate the value of what Nixon and Knight are saying.

The second time I saw Tom was at a later conclave. He was sitting all alone, tying his famous Calcasieu Pig Boat, and we had a very pleasant chat. He told me that after World War II, when the big impoundments were built and the spinning reel appeared, most of his friends gave up fly fishing and switched to the modern tackle that was coming on the market. He didn't enjoy spin fishing, however, and stayed with the fly rod. When Tom was young, fly fishing was restricted to cork bugs and a few outlandish bass flies. His lure-fishing friends were outfishing him badly, an experience with which I can identify. So Tom, a mechanical engineer who is used to solving problems, found ways to modify many casting lures and baits for fly rod use. He told me things that I didn't want to hear, such as: "the top five feet belongs to you," but below that fly fishing gets increasingly difficult. He had plenty of time to talk to me, because all the people were crowded around Jimmy Nix and Billy Munn who were sculpting gorgeous, artistic topwater baits with intricately stacked deer hair. It seemed that the torch had been passed to a new generation of warmwater fly fishers, and Tom's rubber-hackled Pig Boat seemed crude, corny and out of style. I've lived and fished in Texas long enough to know that Tom has probably forgotten more about southern bass than anyone at that meeting might know, but I was imbued with a different emotion. I was really rather sad. I felt a little sorry for this gentleman angler whose time had passed.

Tom's book addresses the whole range of topwater cork and deer-hair flies that were available in his pre-Whitlock era. But when it comes to fish that are not surface oriented, he advocates the use of unweighted spinner baits, fly-spinner combos, spoons, jigs and soft-plastic lures on the fly rod. Bass that are suspended over deep structure or cruising the bottom may occasionally pick up one of those artistically-tied flies for a between-meal snack, but they really don't perform well enough to cut the subsurface mustard on southern lakes. Once he masters Tom's approach, the fly rodder can take fish that had previously been only an elusive dream.

## SUBSURFACE FOOD FORMS

### •BAITFISH•

Largemouth bass predominantly eat fish—any kind of fish, including each other. Some anglers believe that the post-spawn male is only trying to disperse his carefully protected fry for their own good when he charges into them. Wrong. He is indeed trying to eat them. Even larger bass, when confined in close quarters, will attack and try to eat each other. Mr.

Bigmouth would prefer to eat crawfish and salamanders, since they require less effort and provide a
substantial meal, but they simply aren't available in
the necessary quantities. Small sunfish are usually
plentiful, however, and they comprise the most
important item in the diet of pond bass. In larger
lakes, threadfin shad or any one of several open-water
shiners may play the same role. Fathead minnows,
while abundant in many ponds, are still not readily
available to bass in large enough quantity (unless the
lake level is low), due to their defensive behavior of
staying right up against the bank in a couple of inches
of water. Other common and plentiful baitfish, such
as the black-striped top minnow, are of no significance because bass can't catch them.

Pond managers and anglers should bear in
mind that certain trash fish can also be beneficial in
some fisheries. Contrary to common belief, brown
bullhead, called "polliwogs" in many areas of the
South, will not infest a pond if gamefish are present
to control them. The juveniles are easily caught by
bass. I wasn't aware of the forage value of these
apparently worthless little *Ictalurids* and, on the
advice of neighbors, trot-lined them all out of my
ponds to the detriment of the fishery. A healthy bass
population in any body of water requires an equally
healthy breeding population of some kind of forage
fish. Bass aren't fussy about the species as long as
they aren't too hard to catch.

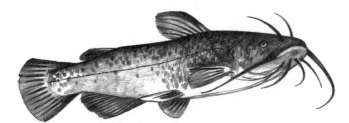

*Called "polliwogs" in
the rural South, brown
bullheads are an
important component
of the diet of large-
mouth bass.*

As I point out in *The Sunfishes*, there are, in
East Texas alone, 22 species of minnows and shiners
(Cyprinidae), thirteen kinds of darters (Percidae), four
silversides (Athernidae), five species of topminnows
(killifishes), two separate shad (herring), one abundant little live bearer (*Gambusia affinis*, the common

mosquitofish), and six small forage sunfish (flier, spotted, banded pygmy, orange-spotted, dollar and bantam). And that doesn't even include the fry and fingerlings of scores of other rough and game fish that inhabit bass waters. Obviously, even the most dedicated match-the-minnow enthusiast can't carry that many imitations, and attempts to do so would be ludicrous, but we can look for certain salient features of individual species. It behooves the serious angler to determine which baitfish are most prevalent in his home water.

Fortunately, it's possible to effectively imitate the profile and behavior of most of these species with bona fide flies, but it's of paramount importance to know what kind of pattern to use at what time. Bear in mind that bass are always opportunistic, unlike the insect-feeding sunfish which can be downright selective at times. If it looks like a vulnerable fish to a bass, and if the bass is hungry, it will take it. It makes no difference if the bass has seen the prey before. You could throw a parrot fish in a pond and, if it's still alive, a bass will still eat it without hesitation. But, if the largemouth finds the parrot fish distasteful in any way, it will never eat another one as long as it lives. The bass has the best memory of any gamefish. The operative word here, no matter how trite and over-worked it may be, is "vulnerable."

It rarely matters whether you present a Pop Lips Pumpkinseed, one of Jim Stewart's plug flies or Bud Priddy's Crippled Minnow to a bass that is lurking in ambush. What matters is that the fly looks vulnerable, like a wounded baitfish. That same bass is more likely to charge one of those "action" patterns than one of my Marabou Muddlers. The latter represents a perfectly healthy fish that is fully capable of getting away, but the former looks like a small fish in trouble. "Why," you might ask, "do I see bass attacking baitfish that seem to be perfectly normal?" After much observation, I know there must be something about that little victim that differs from the others. I can't tell you what, perhaps it seems preoccupied or something else sets it apart. I have watched dozens of juvenile bluegill swim right past the nose of a hiding bass, who watches them intently but does not molest them. Suddenly, for no obvious reason, the bass grabs some hapless individual that seems no different from the others. If we had all the answers it would take the fun out of fishing.

The Marabou Muddler is my "fly of choice" for bass that are chasing minnows in the shallows or schooling on shad in open water, but a Pop Lips pattern will more likely tempt a visible bass lurking in the weeds. Until very recently, fly fishers tended to ignore this aspect of bass behavior because they couldn't get the desired action into their flies. Only a jointed plug or crank bait would entice a hiding bass to ambush, but modern tiers, like Bob Popovics and Jim Stewart, are doing a much better job of building action into their patterns. A standard streamer pattern will not be very effective when cast blind into likely cover, but a wobbly, crippled offering may bring sensational results. When minnow-chasing fish are visible, regular streamers, like a Marabou Muddler, perform very well. My preferences here are personal, but they are the result of many hours on the water.

If a hiding bass refuses all of the above and won't take a surface fly or a streamer, you may want to reconsider your definition of fly rodding and hang a spinner blade in front of the fly. If the bass still won't clobber that, the next step is something like a fly-rod spinner bait or Tom McNally's Spin 'n Strip: a piece of wire with a rotating spinner blade, attached to a single hook baited with a strip of pork rind. If you still can't catch that largemouth, it's time to start thinking about soft plastic.

I rarely see anyone fishing with pork rind anymore. Soft plastic has replaced it. Old timers used to fish with what was called a "pork chunk." It was just a piece of raw pork. As bizarre as it seems today, Jack Knight insisted that it be fresh pork; the cured stuff wasn't as good. An (otherwise respectable) fly fisher even said that, although it wasn't "pleasant to work with," the chunk becomes "a thing of life" in the water. Imagine any fly fishing writer saying such a thing today. I may be going too far with the soft plastic, but at least it's not raw meat. The reason it worked, of course, was not that bass like pork, but the soft texture of the flesh. The popular Jig and Pig, a big plastic worm rigged on a heavy jig, is doubtless a descendant of those baits. I was comforted by the pork chunk though, realizing that no matter how far you sink, there always seems to be someone left to look down on.

### •CRAWFISH •

These abundant crustaceans are second only to forage fish in the diet of stillwater largemouth. The crawfish is very much an American organism that has been heralded as a source of food and recreation in its own right. Of the 500 worldwide species, 350 of them are indigenous to North America. Most American species are quite small and many are entirely terrestrial. The juveniles are exact duplicates of their parents and, unlike their marine cousin, the crab, they do not undergo any kind of metamorphosis. The young grow rapidly and molt (discarding the shell) frequently. They are most attractive to bass during the post-molt stage, which may last for a week, when they are quite soft and delicious. People who tie crawfish patterns with wire and other hard, rigid materials just haven't done their homework.

The red swamp crayfish (*Procambarus clarkii*) has been widely cultured for both bait and food and is common across the South. During the post-molt phase, the young of this species are decidedly olive-green in color, while the juvenile white river crayfish (*P. actutus actutus*), as the common name would imply, are cream or grayish after molting. The young craw-fish molt every few days throughout the spring so they are quite vulnerable much of the time.

*Bass prefer crawfish in the post molt stage.*

Joe Robinson, a superb Texas fly tier and angler, *has* done his homework. It's no accident that he uses soft suede leather for the claws and carapace of his famous Mud Bug. Joe's fly is so realistic that horny Texas crawfish have actually tried to mate with it. Talk about "virtual-reality" sex. This is probably one of the hardest flies to tie, and Joe is still the only one who can tie it correctly (although Don Barbay of Beaumont, Texas ties a reasonably close version).

When former *American Angler* editor, Jack Russell, asked Joe to write an article on the pattern, he found the tying sequences so incredibly intricate that he couldn't possibly use them all in the magazine because there were so many and each one was so complex. The resultant article was excellent, but it didn't teach me to tie the fly. It would probably take several lessons from Joe just to master the basics. Since I've never used a real Mud Bug, I can't say how it works. I would think, however, that it would fish better in the smallmouth rivers of the Texas Hill Country, where Joe fishes, than in weedy lakes. I prefer soft plastic for crawfish imitations because I can drag the fly on the bottom with no fear of snags or moss buildup on the head. The two-inch Soft Craw Jr. from Renegade Bait Company does an excellent job, and they offer it in green to simulate the post-molt juvenile of the red-swamp crawfish.

In smaller, cleaner waters, Gary Borger's Swimming Female Crawfish, tied without the lead weight, fishes credibly well. By and large, however, both crawfish patterns and large nymph imitations are flies for the smallmouth fisher. Harry Murray and Bob Clouser have a lot more use for such flies in their comparatively clean rivers than we do in our weed-cluttered stillwaters.

### •SALAMANDERS•

Salamanders are probably at the very top of the bass's list of food preferences. They are, however, less significant as a source of protein than either forage fish or crawfish because their numbers in a given lake, pond or river tend to correlate inversely to the number of gamefish present. They are most abundant in poorly oxygenated waters, not because they like stagnant water but because there are fewer predatory fish there. In my area, only bowfin inhabit these backwater areas. Since salamanders have no defenses, other than their nocturnal habits, they are quickly eaten when they venture into bass water. Even though these bizarre-looking amphibians may not be present in large numbers in your lake, rest assured that offering a bass anything that resembles one is like offering candy to a baby!

There are five families of salamanders (order Caudata) of interest to anglers, and each is important enough to warrant a brief discussion. My own knowledge of these creatures comes from a summer of observation and collection some years ago when a group of neighborhood children developed a keen interest in aquatic salamanders as a result of a school film they had seen. The youngsters did the wading, dipping and seining while I followed behind with field guides and note pad, doing my best to calm the girls and admonishing one mischievous boy not to throw these ugly creatures into the girls' hair or drop them into their clothing (at least not the Amphumia, because they can bite). It was an educational experience for all of us, and helped me to better understand the warmwater habitat and, especially, the deadly effectiveness of the plastic worm. (The young man who dropped a water dog in his sister's hair just received his degree in biology and is going on to graduate school. I like to think our salamander hunt played some small role in that.)

Some of the species we identified that summer were not indigenous to East Texas, but came from Alabama or the Florida panhandle. It is common to find salamanders outside of their original range because, like crawfish, they have been widely sold and transported as bait for many years. Also, identification is complicated by the fact that species within a family readily hybridize, and I am not sure that our taxonomy was always accurate—but we were close enough for angling purposes.

The most common species are in the family Necturidae, the mud puppies (also called "water dogs" in the South). Plastic baits that imitate them are erroneously called "lizards" by bass fishers (salamanders are all amphibians and not related to lizards, which are reptiles). All five species of Necturids have external gills that fan like ostrich or marabou plumes in the water, and they also have four well-developed legs. Coloration varies from tan to brown and shades of slate-gray to black. They all have distinct, contrasting spots covering both the dorsal and ventral parts of the body. One species, the Dwarf Water dog (*Necturus. punctatus*), is purplish. The Necturids are easily cultured and they are the most popular salamander among live bait dealers.

*mud puppy, or water dog*

In East Texas, we commonly see species of the family Sirenidae. The sirens also have external gills, like the water dogs, but have only one pair of small, short legs right behind the gills, while the Necturids have four legs. Some species are quite large in adulthood. We caught one specimen that summer that was two feet long and let out a shrill cry that scared us half to death. Some smaller sirens are colorful, sporting yellow spots or stripes on an olive background, but one Okefenokee subspecies (of *Pseudobrancus striatus axanthus*), the dwarf siren, is solid brown. The slender dwarf siren (*P. striatus spheniscus*) has two bright yellow stripes on each side of its body, and it measures only a few inches long. Dwarf sirens have migrated along the Gulf Coast from their original home in Florida, along with the hyacinth.

*siren*

Remember this little fellow the next time you fish around rafts of that dreadfully invasive plant and offer the bass a small olive worm. Small worms are even available that specifically seek to mimic the dwarf siren, complete with yellow stripes. Bass fishers study these organisms and attempt to imitate them with the same enthusiasm and sophistication that trout fishers apply to mayflies.

Members of the Salamandridae family, the newts, also have four well-developed legs like the water dogs, but are distinguished by the absence of external gills.

*newt*

The newt spends its infancy in the water as a larva, but soon crawls out as a colorful eft. This eft stage, usually characterized by bright markings to warn predators of the toxins, lasts a year or more and the adolescent animal is entirely terrestrial. The newt then transforms into a drably-marked adult. It then reenters the pond where it breeds and completes its life cycle. Mature aquatic newts have a rust or reddish cast and bass fishers use "strawberry lizards" in lakes that have substantial populations. I used to think that fish didn't eat newts, because of their toxic secretions, but I now believe that the irritating mucus provides less protection in the aquatic phase because I have seen wading birds feeding on newts that are rising to gulp air on the surface—mostly in shallow backwater areas on a hot afternoon.

The Amphumia, like the sirens, also have only a single pair of legs located at the front of the body, although their legs are smaller and less developed. They do not have external gills, which distinguishes them from the Sirenidae which do have visible gills. Most species are too large in adulthood for a bass to eat, but may be important forage in the larval stage. Erroneously called "congo eels" in the rural South, they can deliver a nasty, but non-venomous, bite and should be handled carefully. If you're not sure whether it's a siren or an Amphumia, assume the latter. Fortunately, I read the field guide before venturing forth with my young charges that summer long ago, and, although there was much talk of the possibility, no one was bitten. The most important species of the family, for our purposes at least, is the drably-colored one-toed Amphumia (*Amphiumia pholeter*) which only attains a length of eight to ten inches. It is effectively imitated with a black plastic worm.

Now it gets complicated. The many species of Plethodontidae, or lungless salamanders, do not have visible gills and their four legs are well-developed. It is easy to tell them from the water dogs, because they lack the external gills, but it takes a herpetologist (or at least someone who knows more than I do) to separate lungless salamanders from the newts. I'm guessing when I try to distinguish between the two families. Like the bass fisher says, they're all "lizards." When you see them gulping air, however, they are definitely newts.

Even this brief review of the aquatic salamanders leaves no doubt as to why plastic worms and lizards have always been, and will likely always be, the very best lure for non-feeding, lethargic bass. Warmwater fish are simply unable to resist these creatures. It's an addiction that has been deeply etched on their genes over thousands of years.

Significantly, all aquatic salamanders are carnivores and forage nocturnally for nymphs, snails and the like. The salamanders hide at the bottom in detritus and decaying vegetation by day, where they are safe from all but the most inquisitive bass. This nocturnal activity explains why fishermen find that at night a dark plastic worm works better than a surface lure. Salamanders swim with a "sinusoidal," or side to side, motion that is best mimicked with a soft-plastic lure or possibly, for you diehards, some sort of articulated fly.

A rabbit strip appears to mimic a salamander but, I'm sorry to say, it just doesn't perform like a plastic lizard when fished subsurface. I think this is a function of texture, although the wet rabbit strip seems soft and "chewy" to us, it apparently does not feel lifelike in the bass's mouth, and is quickly ejected. These flies fish superbly on the surface because the fish savagely charges a topwater bait and

strike detection is not a problem. As pointed out
earlier, the bass's underwater take is usually slow
and subtle.

*Four-inch "lizard"
rigged for the fly rod.*

While it's theoretically
possible to imitate these
organisms with flies, it's not
very feasible in actual practice. Once I stopped
worrying about being a fly-only purist and accepted
reality, I started catching more bass on the fly rod
than I ever dreamed possible. I once tied rabbit strip
flies until I was blue in the face but none of them
proved very successful as bottom-crawling imitations.
I either had to accept that fact of life or, to be brutally
honest, forget about being a serious bass fisher.

## PLAN A - SOFT PLASTIC
*"I know that plastic worms . . . are a far cry from most
concepts of fly rod lures, but a bass is also a far cry from the
conventional target of the long rods."*
                                              *Tom Nixon, 1977*

Tom's most valuable contribution may turn out to be
his recognition, albeit reluctantly, that soft-plastic
lures are indeed fishable on the fly rod. He saved that
information for the last chapter and said it "may be
more trouble than it's worth." I'll go farther than Tom
did. Soft plastic imitations of eels, snakes, crawfish
and salamanders are indispensable for the angler who
wants to seriously pursue largemouth bass in
stillwater. I realize that many of my friends are going
to reject my advocacy of these admittedly repulsive
baits (real salamanders are also fairly repulsive). Tom
would have chosen to stay with traditional flies too,
but, as a pragmatist, he did what the problem demanded. In today's vernacular, he "got real." I cautiously broached the subject of plastic lures on fly

125

tackle to Dave McMillan, the big bass champ of Texas fly rodders, several years ago ("I have this friend who says that . . ."). As expected, he stated emphatically that "that's not fly fishing" and he added that I should pick my friends more carefully! I agree that the practice does not qualify as fly fishing so, in deference to Dave, I'll call it *"bassin' with a fly rod."*

The term "fly fishing" is usually defined in one of two ways. The most common definition, that often used by regulatory agencies, describes the fly itself. If you are fishing with a single-hook lure that is constructed of fur and feathers (synthetic materials have complicated this considerably), then you are *legally* fly fishing. By that definition, an angler who spin casts a fly below a bobber is fly fishing. The other definition, the one I prefer, limits the application of the term to "a method of angling whereby the weight of the line is cast rather the weight of the lure." If the lure is castable, if its weight is lighter than the front thirty feet of the fly line (so that it doesn't overpower the line), then the angler is fly fishing. Most modern fly fishers would probably combine the two criteria into a very narrow definition, but to me just being able to use my fly rod instead of the casting rod is rationalization enough. As long as we release our fish unharmed, does it really matter?

I didn't give up easily on deep fly fishing though, and 1991 was my "season of discontent." I was determined to overcome my subsurface problems without compromising my fly fishing principles, but my resistance broke down one lovely September morning. My friend James Ewings and I began the day fly casting size 2/0 hair bugs along the shore of Lake Sam Rayburn. We took a number a nice fish before the hot sun burned out the topwater action. James fired up his big Johnson and ran to a high spot out in the middle of the lake. The bottom rose to twelve feet and was covered with hydrilla, some of which extended to the surface. James put his 10-weight rod back in its tube and rigged a black plastic worm on his casting rod. He took a three pounder on the first cast. I knew what to expect as I threaded the Wet Cel V through the guides. James had another fish on before I tied a size 2 Serpent Fly to the 10-pound tippet.

I had been through this so many times that I just fished mechanically, not expecting to catch anything. I wanted to go home. James's casting rod had broken my spirit long before this day. He was grinning from ear to ear, playing his third fish now. I mindlessly stripped the fly and responded to his whoops of glee with rude suggestions of an anatomical nature. A small bass grabbed my fly a few feet from the boat. I knew from past experience that others had likely done the same while the fly was deeper. I desperately wanted that fish, but I couldn't set the hook because a straight line was impossible that close to the boat. The line was perpendicular to the rod tip and the fish got away. James was rolling in the bottom of the boat, laughing hysterically at my efforts to stick the fish with the fly rod tip. That did it. I'd had enough.

I could have accepted the situation if my flies yielded a few fish once in awhile, but nothing worked for me. I decided that the fellows who wrote articles about these tactics hadn't done much bass fishing, had never tested their concepts in actual practice. I came to believe that at best, these techniques were developed on small, shallow ponds or, at worst, in the library—certainly not on a large Texas bass lake. It struck me more than once that perhaps my own incompetence was the culprit. That may still be true, but I received confirmation through similar reports from other fly fishers who were having the same negative results.

I now recall that some of the magazine articles I had read, describing the sinking-line technique, never mentioned actually catching fish on the high-density lines they were touting. They presented raw, untested theory which I misinterpreted as fact. I had no choice but to concede defeat; to accept the fact that there was no realistically workable fly fishing system that could compete with soft plastic, or even hook enough fish to make it worth the effort.

Developments in conventional fly tying have not solved these problems for me, and I am not optimistic that they will any time soon. Every day, I watch my bass-fishing counterparts use soft plastic and hardware with results that most fly fishers would describe as spectacular. I can no longer deny the fact that their lures are not only more effective, but often their fishing method is the only way to take bass that are not actively feeding. In earlier years, I avoided subsurface bass entirely. If I could not interest them with shallow-water techniques (unless they were schooling on baitfish, or otherwise visibly feeding), I just accepted that and went fishless. And I went fishless a lot. Al McClane understood the limitations of fly fishing for bass; he once cited the fact that of 443 prize-winning bass in the old *Field and Stream* contest, only sixteen were taken on the fly rod. That wouldn't mean much today, but the fly rod was much more widely used in earlier times.

If all of this is true, if our topwater flies are only effective during occasional feeding periods and bass spend most of the time suspended over structure or hugging the bottom under weedbeds, you could conclude, I suppose, that much of the time lake-dwelling largemouth are not appropriate quarry for the fly fisher. Perhaps, some might argue, we should leave them in the domain of the casting rod and fish elsewhere for more cooperative species. That might be a viable alternative for the fortunate few who can afford frequent flights to the Rocky Mountains, but I live in bass country and bass are what I have (and like) to fish for.

I reached the end of my patience that day in James's boat and I was ready to try any alternative. Orthodoxy be damned! I grabbed a hook from his box (without even asking), tied it to the leader butt section, bit a couple inches off a tattered plastic worm that I found in the bottom of the boat and threaded the worm onto the hook. I chunked this thing out there about thirty feet and let it sink. I saw the line moving and found myself connected to a nice fish.

My performance for the next two hours was absolutely unbelievable. James even switched back to his fly rod and joined me, since I was outfishing his weighted worm about four to one. This deadliest of all bass lures became even deadlier when fished without the encumbrance of lead weight—we were able to slither it through the moss in a much more seductive manner than was possible with the casting rod.

Unfortunately, it was a little too deadly. In the

heavy weeds the sinking lines did not telegraph the delicate strikes to our stripping hands quickly enough and too many fish were hooked deep in the gullet, a problem that precluded our ever doing this again. We even had to cut an occasional hook off and leave it in the fish. Both of us recognized that this practice was clearly unsportsmanlike, but the injured bass did not suffer in vain. The experience suggested that the soft, meaty texture of the plastic lure accounted for its success, forcing me to reexamine the most fundamental precepts of my angling philosophy. Assuming that a heavy sinking line was necessary to fish the worm successfully, I gave up the practice and advised others to avoid it. That's where I was in the fall of 1991, when I wrote *The Sunfishes*, but further developments were yet to come.

I concluded, as I told James on the way home, that if these fish were that insistent on soft plastic, then they should have it! (Even the hardest head eventually caves in if you beat on it long enough.) I purchased a casting rod and reel the next day and reluctantly settled for that whenever the bass wouldn't take my bugs and divers. I caught a lot of fish and learned a great deal about bass fishing while using the casting rod, but I neither enjoyed it nor accepted it. I still believed that the problem could be solved at the fly-tying vise and I unsuccessfully searched for material with the right texture.

It's a fact that you won't consistently take non-feeding, subsurface bass on fly tackle unless your offerings appeal to the fish's sense of feel as well as its sense of sight. Texture is the key. You can go another step and apply worm scent, appealing to the fish's olfactory senses, but, as Dave Whitlock discovered at a Texas conclave a few years ago when he advocated the use of Dr. Juice, that's going too far. Anyone who has spent a lot of time on big bass lakes, as Dave and I both have, understands that these fishing problems clearly demand unorthodox solutions. Dave quickly withdrew his advocacy of worm scent and the product disappeared from the L.L. Bean catalog, but I too have experienced the same kind of desperation that must have driven him to "juicing" his flies.

I was preoccupied with the question of texture, as Dave and other fly rodders have doubtless

been. I thought I had the answer when I read about
Bob Popovic's "Siliclone" saltwater flies in *American
Angler*. Bob dubs wool onto the hook shank and coats
it with clear silicone. The result is a soft, rubbery lure
that is similar to molded-plastic baits, although a lot
more rigid and not nearly as weedless. In forming the
plastic onto the hook instead of buying it in a bag at
the tackle shop, the fly tier produces something
"respectable" that qualifies as a "fly." I made a
Siliclone, soaked it in mud and fish slime to get rid of
the strong chemical smell, and fished it deep on the
USL (Uniform Sink Line) at the next opportunity. It
tended to hang in the brush, and the head of the fly
gathered moss, but I did catch fish on this homemade
plastic lure—especially if I applied Dr. Juice to it.
Unfortunately, the fish tended to swallow it just like
the commercially made baits, and it didn't draw
nearly the number of strikes as the manufactured
lures. It didn't fish well enough to justify the effort of
the sinking line, so I continued fishing with the
casting rod.

*A worm must be properly
rigged or it will twist the line.*

Although I found "heave 'n' crank" more
enjoyable than fly fishing without results, every time
I hooked a bass I experienced regret that I wasn't
using my fly rod. The time I spent with conventional
bass tackle did, however, increase my knowledge of
bass behavior, added new tools to my arsenal, enhanced my credibility with other anglers in my area
and gave me a very valuable searching tool on big
waters. I'm glad I learned to use it, but it was always a
last resort. I had accepted, after years of frustration
and effort, that fly fishing is useful only for feeding or
spawning bass that are within a couple of feet of the
surface and I limited my use of the fly rod to such fish
(as my friend James and other sensible warmwater
anglers had always done). One positive outcome was

that, since I had been willing to try their tackle, my bass fishing friends became a lot more openminded about the fly rod. There are three ways to sportfish: bait casting, spin casting and fly casting. The truly competent and versatile angler will learn from all three of them.

The following spring I discovered that there was a way to present plastic imitations on the fly rod after all, without gut-hooking fish. I spent a delightful, but fishless, afternoon guiding two fly fishing friends from Houston on Lake Steinhagen in East Texas. Later, at the launching ramp, we had a very pleasant chat with two personable young men who pulled several beautiful bass from their live well and released them in our presence. We were accustomed to such ego-deflating displays from hard-core bass fishers, but these boys had spinning rods and were fishing six-inch Tequila Sunrise worms with no sinkers. They explained that they cast the unweighted lure at the base of a cypress tree and the bass took it as it slowly sank. On the way home, we all decided that the next morning we would try to fish a smaller version of that lure on our floating lines. We discussed the problem that James and I had experienced with deeply-hooked fish taken on the sinking lines. If that occurred, we vowed to curtail the practice immediately. We spent hours that evening trying to rationalize the step we were about to take, conferring frequently with Jim Beam, and decided that if we could successfully fish this bait on the fly rod without compromising our conservation ethic, why not give it a try?

We didn't need any further rationale the next morning because all three of us had a blast and, best of all, not a single fish—absolutely none—swallowed the bait. The bass clobbered the worm as it sank, just as the boys had assured us, and it was nearly as much fun as fishing a topwater bug. It took considerable skill, too. I felt a little tap (no wonder James and I couldn't detect these strikes with our sinking lines lying on the bottom) and then, after a pause of three or four seconds, the line would tighten. That was the cue to sock it to the fish with the rod butt and line hand. If our timing was right, a gorgeous greenish-bronze largemouth would come flying out of the

water. We were casting normally, we could feel the
delicate take with our line hand and were able to play
the bass by "hand" without a reel or other mechanical
contrivance between us and the fish. It was great
fishing in anybody's book. We were pleasantly surprised that the four-inch worm cast fairly well (easier
than a thoroughly saturated rabbit-strip fly, which we
also tried during the morning without success). The
reality here is simple, obvious and straightforward—
there's no need to deny it anymore—it takes soft
plastic to catch lethargic bass!

Anyone who spends time around skillful bass
fishermen will eventually have to face this fact, but
it's a lot less painful now that the fly rod option is
open. One of my companions that day is (was) something of a purist who always steadfastly refused to use
the casting rod, but he was able to accept the plastic
worm if he could use it on his fly rod. I am afraid that
we are all corrupted beyond salvation—"reprobates"
as the my Baptist neighbors would say.

Quite frankly, that experience completely
changed my angling life. I have worked out most of
the problems and I can now catch bass any time, any
place and release them unharmed. The bass fishermen now outfish me only when the fish are very deep
in the winter months; in fact, I often outfish them
with my floating line and 4-inch crawfish, salamander
or eel.

The secret is the lighter line. Strike detection
was so slow on the high-density line that the fish had
time to swallow the hook. On a floating, sink tip or
intermediate line, I can feel the tap immediately and
have learned with experience just when to strike.

*Strike detection is no problem with an intermediate or sink-tip line.*

Jason Lucas was the first to recognize the subtle nature of the bass's underwater take, but not until he started fishing pork rind slowly on the bottom. Prior to that he assumed that bass took beneath the surface as ferociously as they did on top, because all he had ever observed was an ambushing bass attack a crank bait or spoon. When he began to understand how bass sluggishly cruise the bottom, picking up a crawfish here and a salamander there, he began to fish the pork rind as we fish a plastic worm, even rigging it in a weedless manner as we do today. At this moment, modern bass fishing was born. "A bass's tendency to hang onto a pork rind lure a moment or two is what makes catching him in this manner possible," Lucas observed in the late forties. The plastic worm would not appear until the mid 1950s, although "rubber pork rind" was available at the time of Lucas's discovery. Jason Lucas and Jack Knight both rejected the imitation pork rind. The latter even insisted that his pork rind be fresh and would not use the cured product. Knight, however, never really got a handle on that type of bottom fishing. Lucas is the pioneer there. Other anglers of the pre-plastic period used something called "pork chunks," which was nothing more than a piece of meat. It worked because it felt right in the fish's mouth.

The fish sometimes picks up the plastic bait so delicately that I detect it only by a very slight quivering movement of the tip of the fly line. The angler must understand the extreme subtlety of the bass's underwater take to fish successfully, regardless of the type of tackle used. If fly rodders decide to once again look seriously at these fisheries, someone may develop flies and techniques so we don't have to use soft plastic anymore. I predict that if such a fly is tied it will come from the vise of either Bob Popovics, Tom Farmer or one of their students. Are you listening, gentlemen? I can almost guarantee that future innovations will not involve high-density lines; at least not for soft-bottom, heavily-vegetated waters. I don't see how they could have any ethical future in practical bass fishing in the deep South, but I have a couple of northern friends who are fishing soft plastic on fast USL lines without gut-hooking fish. Their lakes have rocky bottoms and vegetation is minimal by comparison. "North" starts at Dallas and everything beyond the Red River is a foreign country.

A soft-plastic lure should be fished on a very short leader—approximately 3 feet of level mono—unless you need more depth. Bass are not tippet shy, so I often use twenty-pound test Maxima and never go lighter than twelve-pound test. Most lures and flies fish better if they're attached with a loop, but a clinch knot works better here. Sliding the head of the worm over the clinch knot minimizes wind-resistance while casting and helps prevent line twisting while fishing. Rigging the bait on the hook is simple, but it must be done correctly. If it's not straight, the imitation will spin unnaturally and twist your fly line.

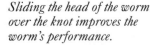

*Sliding the head of the worm over the knot improves the worm's performance.*

These lures should be fished very slowly, just slithered along near the bottom. This is easily accomplished with fly tackle because you have a direct connection and can impart all sorts of tantalizing, lifelike movement. The casting rod angler must use the rod tip to bring the lure to life, so he doesn't have the sensitivity that a fly fisher does by holding the line in his hand. A weighted worm is unpleasant to fish in the moss because the sinker keeps hanging on the stems and the retrieve is very jerky, complicating strike detection. An unweighted worm, on the other hand, is incredibly realistic as it glides smoothly through even the thickest vegetation. James, who is an experienced tournament bass fisher, says there is no doubt the worm fishes better on a fly line and a number of other hard-core bass men have, upon seeing the fly rod worm in action, grudgingly admitted that the fly rod does indeed seem to be the superior tool. They hasten to add, however, that the

small baits used with a fly rod will not entice many
lunker bass. I agree. The casting rod is the best tool
for those seeking trophy fish because, the occasional
exception notwithstanding, really big bass normally
demand a very large lure.

Most people have a tendency to retrieve these
lures much too fast. I patiently inch it along with short
tugs and the bass can't stand it. It drives them crazy.
You can't believe how much fun it is when you feel
that subtle little "tap, tap." Bass also pick up the
plastic lure while it is lying motionless on the bottom.
There are times when longer, faster strips are required, especially with the worm-type baits. Many
strikes occur before any retrieve has commenced (on
the sink, for example) and I wait until the offering
sinks all the way to the bottom before giving it any
action at all. Since there is normally some slack in the
line at this point, such strikes are often detectable
only by a slight movement of the line tip. Occasionally, a bass will take off with it at high speed, nearly
jerking the rod out of my hand. If I'm getting shallow
strikes, when the lure first hits the water, I immediately switch to a topwater bug, diver or slider.

When you feel the initial tap, let the fish take
the worm for a few seconds, until the line tightens
and starts to move. It's likely the fish is holding the
worm by the tail and you have to give the bass a
chance to get the whole worm into its mouth. Then
slam the hook home with everything you've got. Like
James says, "try to pull his face off." It takes a hard
strike to make contact with the bass's jaw but, using
Whitlock techniques, you can strike as hard as the
bass fisher with his short, stiff rod. Don't wait too
long, however, because the fish will surely swallow
the worm. It is better to err on the side of striking too
fast; better to miss the fish than hook it deep in the
gullet. It breaks the heart of all good sportsman to
release a bleeding, injured fish, or one with the hook
still in it.

When the plastic worm first appeared on the
market, fishing writers advised anglers to let the bass
run before setting the hook. They just didn't realize
in those early days that this advice would result in the
needless death of many small fish. When these
writers became aware of their error, many anglers had

already developed the habit and they had a devil of a time reversing the practice. There is much concern over this problem in the bass literature of the late sixties, and A.D. Livingston even suggested, in 1974, that the worm may have to be banned to alleviate the problem. This has all changed today, of course, as bass fishers have learned how to fish the lure properly. Several of them have approached me on the lake, when they saw that I was casting a worm on a fly rod, to lecture me about striking the fish in a timely manner. I respect their concern and I'm glad they are worried about killing fish. Bass fishers are rarely shy, and sometimes even physically threaten other anglers who are behaving in an unsportsmanlike manner. I once called a nearby angler's attention to a minnow dunker who was yanking the hook out of undersized bass, guts and all. This burly bass angler suddenly shouted, "Hey buddy, you kill one more fish and I'm gonna kick your a——!", and I believe he would have done just that. Needless to say, the bait fisher straightened up his act in a hurry. I doubt if this is what fly-casting expert, Mel Krieger, has in mind when he talks about "peer pressure" to encourage catch and release, but it certainly worked.

Learning how to set the hook is critical. To successfully fish any subsurface offering on the fly rod, you must master Dave Whitlock's straight-line technique, maintaining the straight line at all times. I have to really sock it to the fish with the rod butt and line hand in order to pull the hook point through the plastic bait and into the bass's jaw, and any slack at all will thwart that effort. This is probably the most highly skilled aspect of the whole operation and the most important. If the fish takes the bait close to the boat you will not be able to set the hook with the rod tip and your only choice is to ease the worm out of his mouth and quick-release him. Anyone intending to bass fish with the fly rod should attend one of Whitlock's seminars or view his video tape *Fly Fishing for Bass*. Pay close attention to the way he sets a hook, and then practice until it becomes second nature. I can't emphasize this strongly enough. It may be a good idea not to discuss the worm with Dave or the other participants—you may hit a sensitive nerve.

A float tube is somewhat restrictive and

swinging your arms back on a strike can be difficult. This fishing is easier from a boat. Although possible from a tube, it is less convenient and you'll miss more fish. I can tell you one thing: It's nearly impossible to fish with a full sinking line from a tube. Since this method is primarily applicable to bass fishing on large lakes, and rarely necessary in a farm pond, chances are that you will be in a boat anyway.

In addition to the meaty texture, the next best thing about soft-plastic imitations is that they are absolutely weedless, which doubtless accounts for a significant part of their success. If you fish in cluttered, weedy places like I do, you will quickly learn to love this feature. They don't even gather moss on the head as flies do. I can cast them anywhere, into any kind of cover, no matter how heavy or cluttered. Not having to clean weeds off the lure after every cast is a major virtue and goes a long way toward overriding any aesthetic objections to this fishing method. Don't, however, be tempted to cast your lure into places where landing the fish is obviously impossible—it's very unsportsmanlike.

There have been many advances in the manufacture of these baits since Tom Nixon's day. Bass fishermen know everything there is to know about soft-plastic imitations. They can even discuss the chemical composition of the polymers used in their manufacture and the relative merits of injected and hand-poured worms. I know very little about this subject but I do know that they vary widely not only in color, but in density, design and durability. The popular six-inch lure is marginally castable on a ten-weight line but impractically heavy and awkward for fly-fishing gear. Nixon provides instructions in his book on how to cut a large worm down to a castable weight, and states that the small four-inch versions are "anemic looking imitations of imitations" and are too small to entice bigger fish. Perhaps Tom has higher standards about what constitutes a "big" bass, but there have been many advances in soft plastic since his day, and I find today's four-inch baits completely satisfactory.

The typical bait shop in Texas stocks shelf upon shelf of large worms, lizards and crawfish of every conceivable color and description, but may not have any four-inch baits at all. The smaller lures are more popular in northern and western areas, where clear waters require what bass fishermen call "finesse tactics," but you can usually find a small selection at a big discount store, or you can order them from various catalog sources. Some soft plastic is formulated to either sink or float. The sinking version will usually perform better with a fly line, but may also be heavier to cast. There are scores, maybe hundreds of brands of soft-plastic baits. It's a multimillion dollar business and the industry produces an endless variety of plastic lures of every kind, even plastic salmon eggs for trout.

Charles Waterman is, I believe, the only fly fishing writer before me to actually admit to having tried the plastic worm on the fly rod. In *Black Bass and the Fly Rod*, the dean of warmwater anglers made this statement which, I must admit, assuaged my guilt:

"Most fly fishermen for bass have at one time or another tried to cast a plastic worm with a fly rod. In my case it was hard on both the plastic worm and my disposition. Sure it will work. Using a sink tip or a full sinking line, you can lob one of the smaller worms and retrieve it well enough to catch bass, but this turns into a sort of tip toe strip casting and I classify it as a stunt."

Charles Waterman was probably relieved when the worm wouldn't cast,because it had the potential of repudiating a lifetime of fly fishing. Waterman is one of my favorite fishing writers. I sometimes fish a pond that is alongside a busy highway, and I always chuckle at his account of hooking a truck on the backcast while fishing a roadside ditch along the Tamiami Trail. I don't remember which of his many books contains that story; I first read it many years ago. The worm was hard to cast because he probably didn't want to use it in the first place. I can identify with that attitude, because when I first put a worm on a hook it was tantamount to an admission of defeat—a failure that my friend Dave McMillan admirably still refuses to accept and he chastises me for my weakness. Once I got my head straight on this, I found that I didn't have to "lob" or strip cast (flip)

the lure; that it was no harder to handle than one of
Brian Camp's weighted rabbit-strip flies.

It's very easy to sell fly fishers on this system
because everyone likes to catch fish. Most have
responded very favorably, even enthusiastically. I got
a pleasant phone call the other day from Saxon Judd,
a fly fisher from Tulsa, Oklahoma, with good credentials (he was personally trained by Dave Whitlock).
Saxon said that his biggest limitation was catching
non-feeding bass. He could, like all of us, murder 'em
on bugs and divers when they are actively feeding,
but the rest of the time he went fishless. I told him
about the four-inch worm and floating line. He called
me two days later and said that he never had such a
fun day of fishing. He took 30 bass in two hours from
a Kansas lake and not one was gut hooked. He
couldn't find any small worms, so he bit a couple
inches off the bigger baits and they performed just as
well. He said he was so excited that he couldn't sleep
that night, and, this is a direct quote, the experience
"changed my whole life."

I have spoken with Saxon since and he
continues to enjoy great fishing with the worm. He is
experimenting with sinking lines and reports that he
is not having the gut-hooking problem in lakes with
hard, rocky bottoms, even using a fairly high-density
line (he uses a number four sink rate) Uniform
Sinking line. I think the muddy, weedy bottom here
is part of the problem. It reduces any sensation from
the strike. It may be that these lines can be used
responsibly with soft plastic in some types of waters,
but proceed very cautiously. It's better to err on the
side of conservatism.

I am still experimenting with various lines and
this system is still evolving. I have discovered that I
can use a very heavy sink-tip line, with a 6-inch per
second sink rate, if I cut the tip back to 3 or 4 feet
long. This will deliver the worm to the bottom in 15
feet of water and sensitivity does not seem to be
compromised. The goal is to use as heavy a line as
possible without gut-hooking fish. This method of
bass fishing is completely undeveloped and I am
looking forward to hearing from other anglers as they
experiment with different lines.

## PLAN B - SPINNER BAITS

*"These simple to make, easy to use, productive lures are a
real breakthrough for the serious fly rodding bass fisherman."*

*Tom Nixon, 1977*

Ron Knight still makes fly-rod size spinner
baits and I have quietly fished with them for a long
time. They are indispensable in murky water and on
certain creeks where the bass won't take anything
else. Largemouth hate current and hug the bank.
They will dart out into the stream to grab Ron's little
spinner bait, but, at the same time, they will ignore
any fly that I drag past them. I have found nothing
else that even approaches Ron's lure on local creeks.
Interestingly, Charles Waterman points out that the
Shannon Twin Spinner, an old fly rod lure, was the
"obvious ancestor of the modern spinner bait." Bass
fishers don't realize that many of their lures and
techniques are based on ideas originated by fly
fishermen a century ago. John Alden Knight used
spinner blades regularly, but did not seem to be aware
of the lure to which Waterman refers. He preferred
small metal lures like the Tin Liz, Dardevle and the
Johnson Silver Minnow. He and Bergman both
rejected the miniature plugs that were invented about
1912, but only because they were hard to cast. It is
important to remember that our tackle is far superior
to anything that was available to them, and we can
cast many things they could not.

When the lake is off-color or when bass are
too lethargic to respond to a fly, the spinner bait still
draws many strikes and may save the day. Sinking
bass flies, as lovely to behold as they are, just won't
draw a fish out of the structure unless you put it right
under its nose. Bass that are suspended over flooded
timber at, say, fifteen feet will rise up to five feet to
snatch a whirling spinner but frequently ignore an
Eelworm or Water Pup at the same depth.

This is an intermediate step, to be used when
topwater fly fishing is not producing but you are not
yet desperate enough to resort to soft plastic. All
kinds of fish take this lure. Sometimes bass move into
the shallows on pretty winter days to bask in the sun,
but they ignore any kind of fly. Nothing is more

frustrating than watching a four-pounder lazily finning in two feet of water while your fly slides right past its nose. The spinner bait seems to anger bass, and even a lethargic fish may readily attack it.

There is nothing subtle about this lure and strike detection is no problem.

*Brass bead or lead eyes help to keep the hook in an inverted, snag resistant position.*

I retrieve spinner baits fairly fast, with long, steady pulls. The spinner bait quickly sinks to virtually any depth desired, but if allowed to sink to the bottom it will hang up on weeds or brush.  Since the fish almost always hooks itself on a spinner bait, it can also be retrieved by moving the rod tip when fishing in close situations—a great advantage on a creek or along brushy shorelines where the bow-and-arrow cast is called for. This lure can also be "skittered" effectively in tight situations using the same ancient techniques as the earliest settlers. The lure handles quite nicely on a floating line. You don't need a sink-tip line because the spinner bait sinks like a rock and will pull any line down with it. The blade offers resistance, making it hard to lift out of the water, so retrieve it all the way in before making your pick-up. Novice casters may have a little trouble casting this, as with any fly rod lure, because a double haul is necessary to generate enough line speed. A proficient caster will be able to handle it with ease on 8-weight or heavier tackle.

## PLAN C - JIGS

Fly fishers have accepted this ancient lure for a long time, and it doesn't entail the same philosophical problems as using plastic lures and spinner baits. Many experienced anglers agree that if they had only one lure to fish with it would be a jig, because it is universally effective for all kinds of gamefish. Many fly patterns are essentially just different types of jigs.

Small jigs are ideal for the beginning fly fisher. They work anywhere, anytime for just about any species of fish. They are easy to cast, cheap to buy and a three-year-old child can tie one. You just can't go wrong with a jig. Only a soft-plastic lure is more effective for bass. My friends, Doug Ming and Fred Bunch, regularly fish a membership lake near Houston. This lake is heavily fished and it can be tough, but they consistently do well with a Clouser Minnow, which is essentially a jig. Since it rides keel style, like all jigs do, it is fairly weedless. They also retrieve it quite rapidly, so it won't sink too deep, and take a lot of fish on the speedy retrieve. In my own experience, these lures fish better slowly, but I think that must be a matter of personal style to some extent because Doug and Fred both do very well.

The tiny 1/64-ounce jig head that is available from most fly fishing suppliers—the kind with the fine-wire, plated hook—is comfortable to cast on all but the lightest tackle and will get down into deep structure. It quickly sinks the entire length of the leader and then continues sinking at a slower rate, dragging the floating line down with it. You can easily present this excellent baitfish imitation to bass suspended at twelve feet, or deeper. When snagged, the light hook will straighten as you pull to free it (if you use a stout tippet) and it is easily bent back to its original shape. You may lose a big bass because of this, but the ability to free the jig from frequent snags is worth the risk. A small jig fishes better on a floating fly line than on conventional monofilament because depth can be controlled without using a fast retrieve. Few lures are more effective than a slow-moving jig bouncing tantalizingly through the weeds. I some-times outfish my "heave 'n' crank" companion with it. If you hear the term "leadhead" fly, it's just a euphemism for a diminutive jig.

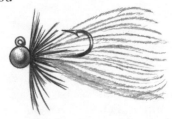

*A small jig is often the best fly rod choice for deep-feeding bass.*

I dress jigs with marabou and, maybe, a little hackle wound over the thread windings. Any color will work, but red-and-white is consistently productive. When there's no topwater action, troll one along the drop-off while kicking very slowly in a float tube or drifting in a boat. When you catch a fish, stop and work the area. Anything that eats minnows and fry will hit this lure—bluegill, bass, channel catfish and especially crappie. I can really do a number on deep crappie with a red/white jig, often hooking one on every cast. Sometimes, I "yo-yo" it straight up and down, simply dapping into holes in the dense summertime moss. The deadliest jigging technique is to bounce it off the trunk of a flooded tree and let it free-fall through the water column. Bass lay up against these stick-ups and will take the jig as it sinks. The jig is a more subtle offering and will not entice sluggish fish like soft plastic or a spinner, but it's very effective for deep, feeding fish.

One memorable morning, I drove a bass fishing friend absolutely crazy with a yellow mini jig. The bass were bottom feeding in flooded timber, probably on their own fry, and his purple worm just didn't "match the hatch." The poor guy suffered the ultimate indignity—getting sacked by a "perch-jerker." If the fish are not active you will likely need to add the spinner to draw strikes.

I admit that I would feel guilty using lures under conditions that are suitable for fly fishing. I hope I never get to the point where I cast a worm to bass that are willing to take a bug, but my angling life is considerably simpler these days. In addition to my box of bugs, divers, sliders and streamers, I carry a lure box containing four-inch plastic baits, #1 worm hooks, various light jigs and a few small spinner baits. When my flies go unmolested, I break out the alternative box and often start catching fish right away. I try to be prepared to switch back to real fly fishing quickly. The other day, I was forced to use a Soft Craw during a slow afternoon and took a number of nice fish. Shortly before dusk, bass started clobbering the bait the moment it hit the water and at the very end of the retrieve, sure signs that they were more surface oriented. I switched to a Grinnel Fly, on the same heavy tippet, and took four more bass on top before darkness fell. It is very important to maintain this kind of flexibility.

Pragmatism demands that I adopt these proven techniques. Tom Nixon does not call this "fly fishing" and neither do I, but I'm having a ball and not harming the fish. Best of all, I'm able to catch bass consistently, in big lakes, without having to use a casting rod. I call it "bassin' with the fly rod," but I do admit that, as Dave McMillan might paraphrase the great Bard, "stink weed by any other name doth smell as foul."

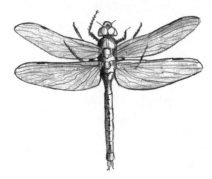

# CHAPTER SIX

## THE RIGHT STUFF

Fly fishing in heavy weeds and flooded timber requires a stout rod, a heavy tippet and, more importantly, a tranquil and composed frame of mind. When I take a Western trout angler to these waters he usually starts cursing the trees and becomes agitated by the constant hang ups, snags and weeds. An Easterner, however, is more accustomed to watching his backcast and adjusts more easily to the cluttered conditions. The more experience the trout fisher has had on small, brushy streams the quicker he will learn the warmwater ropes. Bow-and-arrow casts, steeple casts and plain old "dapping" is often called for here and in such tight habitat stealth and delicacy, the hallmarks of coldwater angling, serve him well.

Dave Whitlock says to play a bass "with authority." In this kind of habitat, you do indeed have to "horse" the fish. A powerful 8-weight outfit and at least a 12-pound tippet is minimal in timber and weeds. Although it's more awkward in heavy cover, I prefer a long rod for the additional leverage. Forget the reel, there's no time to pick up line. Keep the rod tip high, strip as hard as you can, and use all the power you have to keep the fish on top of the weeds or away from the brush and timber.

Using light tackle in mossy areas is unethical because a fish may tangle and suffocate with its gill flaps pressed shut. I have received embarrassing reprimands from bass anglers, most of whom are catch-and-release fanatics, for playing fish too lightly. Now, I often use a twenty pound tippet.

### RODS AND REELS
My Diamondback 8-weight rod is the epitome of what a bass bugging rod should be. I have tried

numerous rods (fly fishers always have to cast each other's rods), but they all feel "funky" compared to mine. Don Davis of Diamondback explained to me that this particular model rod is built with a great deal of power in the butt to lift fish and push big flies. It ends in a very quick, short taper, designed to load only at the very tip end. The fast taper delivers a lot of energy in a hurry, allowing me to develop sufficient line speed to deliver a big bug on target with a crisp, tight loop. I have never cast any other heavy bass rod that performs like my Diamonback, but it is likely that this particular rod simply matches my casting style. It could well be that my rod would feel "funky" to some other caster.

The reel is of no consequence. It's just a place to store the fly line. I don't want to use a reel, however, that is so poorly machined that the leader gets caught between the spool and the housing, or one that makes a lot of noise, is too heavy, or too small to hold the line. Beyond that, I'm not concerned with the reel, nor do I switch spools anymore. I just buy several inexpensive reels to hold various lines.

## LINES

The fly line is, of course, the most important component in the system and I buy only the best. Scientific Anglers now has a line on the market that would be perfect for the type of lure fishing discussed in Chapter Five . . . if it were offered in the larger sizes. Their Mastery Stillwater line is clear, like their Monocore line, but, since it is designed for coldwaters, it does not have the memory problems experienced with those saltwater lines. The "slime" line, as it is known, works great in warm weather, but in cooler waters from late fall to early spring, the very time when I need this line the most, the Monocore becomes too stiff and "springy" to comfortably use, so I have to settle for a regular intermediate or sink-tip line. The Stillwater model has less of a memory problem, and can also serve as a floating line if dressed with silicone. Best of all, these lines are smaller in diameter than conventional lines, alleviating the problems associated with casting in the stiff breeze that always seems to be blowing on a large lake. Before you get too excited, you should know that there's a catch. At the time this is being written (early 1994), the Mastery Stillwater line is not available in the heavier line weights required for this kind of fishing. While the line is perfect for bream and small bass in farm ponds, it can't be used for serious bass fishing on southern impoundments because it is not offered in a size heavier than a 7-weight. There's no way to fish for bass with a 7-weight fly line. They won't handle heavy lures, spinners and jigs, or most bugs for that matter. So, for the time being, we will have to stay with the floating, sink-tip and, in the summer, Monocore lines, at least when fishing big waters.

## LEADERS

The trout fisher needs to make a number of attitude adjustments when it comes to serious bass fishing. While coldwater flies, tackle and methods are eminently applicable to insect-feeding bream, bush-whacking largemouth demand very different techniques. It took a long time for me to accept the fact that bass are rarely tippet shy, but I now understand the reasons why such an obviously intelligent fish is so eager to grab a fly tied to a very visible tippet, while the bluegill is just the opposite and often demands trout-like refinement in terminal tactics. Bluegill can afford to subject their small, relatively immobile prey to a close and often lengthy inspection. The bass's ambush-feeding style does not permit such luxury. When a bass makes that light-ning-quick charge, it is committed and will not be deterred by a bulky tippet.

    I do a lot of lily-pad fishing with big flies using an obscenely heavy tippet (Mason Supersoft, .018", 20 lb. test). My confidence in the heavy tippet has increased. The 1X material (12 lb. test) that I previously used is strong enough to hold a good fish, but it will not withstand the fraying caused by the bass's sandpaper-like teeth. When the fish is hooked inside the mouth, strength is not the only consideration. The tippet must also be *large* enough to hold up to that abrasion. Remember, you cannot allow these fish to run. If the bass "gets its head," the result will be a hopelessly snarled fish. The tackle is under great stress and any weak link will give way when a large bass makes those short, powerful surges toward the cover.

I have learned to stoically accept "the big one that got away," but I lost one last year that really hurt. My friend, Dallas angler Jeff Hines, had his camera loaded and ready when I hooked a fine fish (definitely over five pounds) in fallen timber. I really needed the photograph to illustrate a magazine article and was striving to avoid mistakes, but when Mr. Bigmouth made that inevitable all-out charge toward the safety of the timber, the tippet snapped. It was a brand new 6' bass leader that tested at ten pounds, but the failure wasn't the leader's fault, it was mine for not having retied the knot after taking several fish. The broken end was badly frayed, leaving little doubt as to the cause. If you become complacent about this, the way I did, you may also lose an important fish.

If bass aren't tippet shy, then why not use the heavy tippet all the time? Those of us who carry trout baggage lack confidence in a visible tippet and when we are not raising fish, which is most of the time, we are tempted to refine the terminal gear. I have been doing a lot of closeup bass fishing recently, stalking and observing an individual fish for some time before presenting the fly. I've observed that the bass scrutinizes the prey from a distance and, unless I show myself or retrieve the bug in an unnatural manner, it will not be deterred once it is focused on the offering. You can almost feel the primitive response building—see it in the eyes and demeanor—before the attack. The take is ferocious. I try to raise its head immediately in order to grab a hold of the lower lip, and release the bass before he gets tangled up, and possibly injured. Delicate trout tactics are often required to take midge-sipping bluegill, but not when fishing for largemouth.

Remember to retie the fly to the leader after every fish, be prepared to lose a lot of flies (again, avoid stainless hooks and crimp the barbs) and keep your emotions under control. I have friends who just can't stand to lose flies or fish and their anger unfortunately spoils the experience for them. Learning to tie flies is an economic necessity for the serious warmwater enthusiast.

CASTING

Long casts only aggravate the problems of fishing
cluttered habitat and it is much better to approach the
fish rather than laying a long line over a tangle of
brush or a mass of weeds. Precise accuracy is often
required, especially on the backcast, and few fish will
be brought to net through 50 feet of dead trees or lily
pads. Fish a short line, emphasizing stealth and
concealment, and save the showmanship for lawn
casting. I sometimes find it necessary to overload the
rod by two or three line weights to cast large bugs
and divers in tight quarters. Yes, I have broken rods
doing this.

Every angler knows someone who can cast
outrageously well. They can handle an unbelievable
amount of line with perfect timing and beautiful,
graceful form—and make it look disgustingly easy.
For years I emulated the "poetry in motion" demon-
strated on the casting lawn and wasted hundreds of
hours practicing in private. I was able to place the fly
ninety feet away, even with some accuracy, but only
with Herculean effort—my shoulder ached, I gasped
for breath through clenched teeth and flushed
cheeks. I once bit my lip and drew blood. It became
painfully apparent that I would never adroitly handle
that much line; that no amount of practice would
make me a "pretty" caster.

Really good casters are born, not made. The
requisite hand-eye coordination was determined nine
months before you were born and no amount of
instruction or equipment can change that. I once
asked casting champion and instructor Joan Wulff if
she agreed with that statement. She did, but she
hastened to add that anyone with normal coordination
can learn to cast credibly well. Your natural coordination determines, I believe, the level of skill you can
achieve and my attempts to surpass my own innate
abilities were futile and counterproductive.

Some beginning students at clinics are casting
credibly well in a matter of minutes, while others
struggle for months and still can't make a decent loop.
My inquiries have revealed the not surprising fact
that the talented students invariably shoot par in golf,
bowl in the 200's and earned a letter in high school. I
never broke 100 during my brief golfing career (and

that was on a nine-hole course!) or bowled over 150, and quit trying out for sports in the seventh grade. While a lack of athletic ability obviously precludes tournament casting, my fellow uncoordinated anglers can take heart in the fact that it will in no way hamper their enjoyment of fly fishing, or even decrease their angling effectiveness. We may never be able to show off on the casting lawn or merit the admiration of our peers, but we can all achieve sufficient competence to put the fly where we want it (within a reasonable distance). I fish every day and never worry about casting any more. The rod has become an extension of my arm and I have compensated for the fact that I have a lousy arm by developing other angling skills—stealth, finesse and "fish savvy"—in the same way that a blind person develops exceptional hearing. If you're not such a great caster, don't let it get you down. I am about as uncoordinated as a person can get and if I can fly cast, anyone can.

I think we spend too much time talking about casting and too little time fishing. People tend to get bogged down with a lot of technical information, even physics and such, that really has no application to actual fishing situations. Little of that mumbo jumbo can be translated to the student's hand. Rather than

conduct casting clinics on the lawn, I have decided
that the way to teach beginners to cast is to simply
explain the basics, show them how to hold the rod,
and then send them fishing. All of this reading,
watching videos and listening to lectures does not
teach anyone to cast. If anything it confuses people
and drives them away. It's counterproductive. I have
learned that students become proficient much more
quickly if they simply take a balanced outfit to the
stream or pond and go fishing. After a few days of
frustration, everyone develops their own style and
techniques, which may not be according to any rules,
but they work and that's all that matters. The begin-
ner then knows the object of the game and the
fundamentals of how it works. That's all he needs to
know, and watching the guide or instructor show off is
not helpful. A well-coordinated, athletic person will
grasp fly casting in a couple of hours of fishing.
Someone else may take longer, but they will all
become credible casters if you leave them alone.

The important thing is that you start with a
properly balanced outfit. Many an aspiring angler has
given up in frustration, thinking he could never fly
cast, when the problem was mismatched equipment.
That's where the schools and books do the most good.

All they can teach you is the object of the game and what tools you need, you must teach yourself how to cast. If you were the clumsiest kid on the block you will probably never be a tournament caster. But, you can still learn how to fish with the best of them.

Beginners should go fishing by themselves—they will do much better if allowed to concentrate on the fish without distractions. All that matters is getting the fly to the fish, and regardless of what you tell the novice, he is most likely to develop the same style anyway—one that is natural and comfortable to him. The most important thing about casting is to forget about it. The surest way not to catch fish is to think about your casting. Many times I have watched a student from a distance who was having a horrible time and then suddenly their casting would improve dramatically for a few minutes only to deteriorate once again. That few minutes of credible casting proves that the student is capable of success, so why the inconsistency? When the person gets mentally involved with the fishing and forgets about his casting, you see, he relaxes and the casting improves.

Eight-weight tackle is minimal for casting big bass bugs, plastic worms or spinner baits, and a 9-weight outfit may be better. Some of the soft-plastic lures discussed in Chapter 5 are heavy for fly casting but no more so than many weighted flies. The eel, snake and worm imitations are more aerodynamic than lizards, salamanders and crawfish, so they're easier to cast. I find that the soft-plastic stuff all casts pretty well. Spinner baits and jigs give me more casting trouble. Like a heavily-weighted fly, metallic lures fall so quickly at the end of the backcast that I must start the forward cast before the line completely unrolls, causing me to lose a lot of line speed. While you may not be able to make sharp, crisp casts with perfect, tight loops, the worms and lizards really aren't as bad as you might suppose. Your timing will have to slow down but, after a little practice, you can comfortably fish 50 or 60 feet with no strain at all. You should know how to "haul" the line, because casting the heavier, wind-resistant lures requires the higher line speed created by "hauling." No heavy offering is pleasant to cast, but this is no worse than handling a weighted nymph on a 5-weight. I wouldn't recommend putting a plastic worm on the line when you are trying to demonstrate your casting skill and grace, but it works for practical fishing. If you're a proficient caster you won't have any trouble adjusting to it, but a novice should learn basic casting with ordinary flies before attempting this kind of fishing.

I use regular weight-forward lines, but I think a bass-bug taper would help a lot in this case. Never use a fast sinking line with soft plastic lures. A short sink-tip line is all right and a monocore line works very well—as long as you stay alert to feel the initial "tap" the moment it occurs. I like to be able to switch back to topwater flies quickly if conditions change, so I prefer to stay with a floating line if possible. Bass holding deep may require the use of an intermediate monocore or sink-tip line.

Time on the water is too precious to waste. Lighten up. Relax. Go fishing and just let your casting style evolve naturally. Your concentration should be riveted on the fish and if you dwell on the casting you probably won't catch any. Stay within your "comfort range" and try to refrain from profane self-condemnation when you untangle a tailing loop, slap the water on the backcast or lose a fly in a tree. Don't lose sight of the major objective: going fishing, catching fish and, above all, having fun.

### WHAT ABOUT BOATS

As fly fishers have expanded their interest to saltwater, big western rivers and large lakes, they have reluctantly accepted the reality that many of these waters are accessible only with a boat of some kind. We are steeped in the traditions of a sport that has been practiced while wading in running water and anything less is aesthetically flawed. I too prefer to wade whenever possible and use flotation devices only because it's not feasible to wade many southern waters. To any real fly fisher a power craft is a necessary evil but, unless the warmwater fly fisher restricts himself exclusively to small ponds, he'll need a boat with an outboard motor.

I used to pull a 12-foot jon boat around big impoundments with a set of oars. It was great exercise to be sure, although it became a little embarrassing when well-meaning bass fishermen, assuming that I couldn't afford a motor, would stop to ask if I needed a tow. It wasn't long before I bought a 5-horsepower outboard motor, which was a waste of money because it still took too long to get where I wanted to go, and it didn't have enough speed to safely get me to the bank when the weather turned foul. The 12-foot boat was too small to carry my float tube and/or Kikk Boat and it was too crowded with two people. I soon invested in a commodious 18-foot aluminum boat with a 30-horse motor. I can haul all the gear I want, carry two other anglers with me and, at 25 miles per hour, I can safely go anywhere. I did make one mistake, however, which I hope you won't repeat. Not wanting the burden of keeping a battery charged, I bought a pull-start motor. The motor is just too big to start that way, especially when it's cold or gets flooded, and turning over that big motor with a rope is arduous to say the least!

I didn't trade in my little jon boat. It still has a place in my fishing and I use it whenever and wherever I can. My choice of craft depends on the nature of the water. In a descending scale, I prefer: 1) wading or fishing from the bank, 2) the float tube or Kikk Boat, 3) the small jon boat and 4) the big power boat when none of the other choices are feasible. The serious bass fly rodder should have all of these options available.

## THE VERSATILE JON BOAT

*Nearly every pond has an old jon boat somewhere on the bank.*

Nearly every farm pond has an old square-end, flat bottom jon boat somewhere on the bank. Many anglers prefer the jon boat over the float tube because it's convenient. With some caution and experience, you can stand up while fishing and avoid the hassle of suiting-up in waders, fins and all of the tubing necessities. Some people are just not comfortable in a tube for a variety of attitudinal and physical reasons, including the fear of snakes and alligators, problems with leg cramps and back pain and the universal resistance that people have to anything new or different. Increasingly, native Southerners are rediscovering the fly rod, but they tend to take a dim view of the float tube and insist on continuing to fish from their trusted and familiar jon boat

It's a lot easier to jump in a boat than to get harnessed up in all that float-tube gear and a flat-bottom craft does provide a stable casting platform. But, unless you have someone to paddle for you, you must either anchor the boat, learn to fish and paddle at the same time or be quickly blown against the leeward bank by the slightest breeze. An electric trolling motor is not, in my opinion, a viable alternative. The battery is too heavy to lug around and may get acid on the fly line, the motor is constantly snagging the shooting line (even if you put a net over it as Lefty Kreh suggests) and, worst of all, the whirring noise reverberating through the metal hull will send every fish in the pond scurrying for cover. Don't let anyone tell you that trolling motors don't scare fish. I can prove that they do!

Unless it's blowing a gale, a light anchor, such as a single brick, will suffice to hold the boat while you fish a stretch of shore line, a fallen tree or other structure. I often fish from an anchored boat and it does have one important advantage: it forces me to slow down and work each section of habitat. The mobility of a float tube or Kikk Boat aggravates my number one problem: moving too fast and passing by many fish and much likely habitat. The best bass fishermen may spend all day along a few hundred yards of shoreline, repeatedly fishing probable haunts.

When two anglers share the same boat, it's best to take turns fishing and paddling. My friends and I normally switch over after every fish or two. You can informally play it by ear. (We have been known to argue over the definition of "fish." Does a little bream count? How about one that got away?) I have a friend who hires a young boy to paddle for him and I tried to train my wife to do that job. I never could convince her that it's just as much fun to watch someone else catch a fish, so she didn't work out. A jon boat paddles as well from either end and there's no need to change seats when switching from fishing to rowing. Above all, make sure the paddler wears a hat for protection from those big bass hooks.

Most farm ponds have an old jon boat somewhere on the bank. It may be long unused and full of rainwater, overgrown with vines and weeds or infested with fire ants or even snakes. If you ask permission, the owner will likely indicate that you are welcome to use the boat. There will be no paddle in the boat, so always carry your own. A four-foot-long paddle is my choice. Don't count on anything being in the boat except dirt, water and snakes. If the boat is upside down, turn it over with care since a family of cottonmouth may have set up housekeeping underneath it. It is advisable to tape two six-inch sections of carpet or foam to your paddle, spaced at the right distance to allow you to lay it down quietly on the gunwales. Any banging in the boat will spook the whole pond.

You may want to try old-style "splat fishin", especially if you are fishing alone. This requires you to fish with one hand and paddle with the other. Stand in the forward compartment (between the bow and the front seat) with your feet against each chine, maintaining a wide stance until you find your "sea legs." A jon boat is most easily controlled from the bow. Grasp the paddle with your left hand, about 18 inches from the handle. This choking grip will allow you to brace the paddle against your forearm. Then, with a lot of practice, learn to "scull" with a twisting motion of the wrist and arm. Your right hand is still free to cast and fish.

Once you've mastered the sculling technique, work out no more than 30 feet of line and "splat" the bug into likely spots as you move slowly along the bank. Use at least an 8-weight line and the stiffest rod in your collection, because you must pop the bug and set the hook with the rod tip. The splat fisher used to cut a foot off a standard rod to make it stiffer. An automatic reel is a great help in "one-handed" fishing. In fact it's the only type of fly fishing I have seen where this type of reel offers any advantage. I warn you, this ain't easy! It requires a lot of practice. Indeed, even the most competent fly fisher can be reduced to a bungling neophyte during a first attempt at one-handed fly fishing. It may have come naturally to Grandpa, who fished that way from childhood, but don't expect to master it for a while. There are few splat fishers left to teach us. Most of the old timers who fished this way are in a rest home or the cemetery!

Most anglers prefer to fish while seated in the boat and need to learn to scull and fish with one hand from a sitting position. A shorter, two-foot paddle works best while seated. If you are right handed, sit on the bow seat sideways, that is straddling it, facing the starboard (right) side of the boat. Scull directly over the bow with your left hand. If you are left handed, change hands and face the port side. In either case, you will only be able to fish on one side of the boat unless you are ambidextrous.

Just as the serious warmwater angler needs several different outfits of varying weights, there is no single water craft that is suitable for all situations. I have a tube, a Kikk Boat and a small jon boat in addition to my big power boat and I use all of them regularly. There may appear to be some duplication between the jon boat and Kikk Boat, but sometimes I venture deep into swamps, lily-pad fields or weedbeds where the big boat would be awkward and hard to handle, and the Kikk Boat would not provide sufficient room for all my gear. I carry several outfits, drinking water, food, a first aid kit and a rain poncho. I need to stand up and straighten my arthritic back occasionally, and the Kikk Boat is too confining for sustained comfort over a long period. Moreover, late season vegetation is often too thick for anything other than a light, shallow-draft boat propelled with a push pole, and neither the tube nor Kikk Boat is safe on heavily-traveled public waters after dark.

Aluminum boats come in every size and weight, from light weight ten footers to heavy-duty work boats, and you should consider a number of

factors before purchasing one. First, how will you
transport it? If it is going to be trailered, the boat's
weight and size are less important than if carried on
top of a car or in the back of a pickup. Secondly, some
waters require a narrower beam to get through, for
example, thick stands of cypress trees or flooded
timber, so a wide boat would be a handicap. A wide
boat is easier to pole while a narrow one works better
with oars or a paddle. Finally, the method of propul-
sion must be considered. Some hulls perform better
under power (talk to a knowledgeable dealer about
that). I use a 12-foot boat of standard width that
weighs about 70 pounds. Smaller, lighter models are
available, but they damage very easily, tend to be
unstable and won't safely accommodate two anglers.
My jon boat rides nicely in the back of a standard size
pickup and is light enough to unload and drag to the
water by myself.

While we are inundated with advertising for
every conceivable fly fishing accessory (and some that
are inconceivable), we receive very little information
about boats. Many fly fishers know what a drift boat is
and have used some sort of personal flotation device,
but that's about it. As warmwater fly fishing grows,
the boat manufacturers will begin to address our
unique needs. Until then we are on our own.

If you have to launch far from the fishing area,
you will need a  gasoline motor. An electric motor is
adequate for short distances, but a paddle serves as
well. A jon boat may be sculled over the bow or
transom, but does not handle well when paddled on
the side. If you don't have a motor, keep your eye on
the wind. You may not be able to paddle against it
when it's time to return to your vehicle. Never paddle
downstream on a tailwater. If they start generating,
you may not get home for days! The current swell
from the rising water is much more than you can
handle in a small, motorless boat. It is much safer to
have an outboard motor unless you are intimately
familiar with the area.

When you get into thick vegetation—where
the bass live—you will have to propel the jon boat
with a push pole. I don't like those poles with the
hinged feet that you see in catalogs, they gather too
much moss and weeds. I prefer the fiberglass roller-

extension handle used by house painters. Available from the neighborhood paint store, it extends to twelve feet and the flexibility helps to maneuver the boat. When using it fully extended, I secure the ferrule with a hose clamp or duct tape so it won't slip when I put pressure on it. It sticks in the mud once in awhile, but that's a minor inconvenience. The pole also serves as a temporary mooring if you stick the threaded end into the mud and tie the boat to it. Poling does require some new skills, but they are easily mastered with practice. Always push from the middle of the transom.

Most of us older fellows have a certain amount of lower back trouble and a jon boat thwart is not comfortable for long. A regular padded boat seat is a must for us. Do not, however, attach it permanently unless you trailer the boat because the added weight will make it harder to load and unload. Simply cut a piece of half-inch plywood about 16 inches wide and slightly longer than the beam (width) of the boat. Cut 2 stringers from a 2"x2", each long enough so that when they are placed widthwise the ends touch the inside of each gunwale. Nail these to the bottom of the plywood to provide rigidity and prevent the plywood from slipping off the gunwales. Bolt the boat seat to the plywood and you will be able to remove the seat when you wish. This provides a higher seat with good back support.

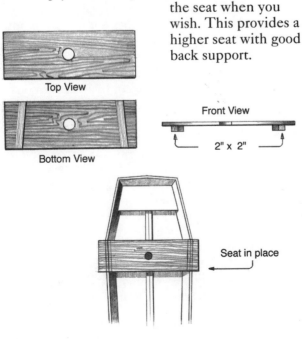

Top View

Bottom View

Front View

2" x 2"

Seat in place

159

You may have noticed that canoes are conspicuous by their absence in this discussion. While very popular among young fly fishers and extremely well-adapted to the conditions we are discussing here, they are tantamount to a medieval torture chamber for older people with bad backs. A cane seat helps a little, but I have to stand up once in awhile. My last canoe trip, seven or eight years ago, nearly killed me!

There are beat up old jon boats scattered all around East Texas. They are a dime a dozen and people don't steal them; they just use them and put them back—but not always where they were found. (We don't chain them to a tree. I tried that once and returned to find it shot full of .22 holes! I failed to respect the local custom and paid the price.)

## BASS BOATS, ETC.

Most fly fishers put big, high-powered bass boats in the same category with "monster" trucks. I sometimes fish with a friend who has a beautiful twenty foot model, powered by a smooth, quiet, 200-horsepower motor and equipped with every comfort imaginable. I have to admit that this thing is a delight to fish from. It has large open decks, comfortable chairs, even stereo sound (all country-western, of course) and a telephone so he can keep in touch with the office. It rides on a four wheel trailer and is easy to tow and launch. It tears across the lake at 50 miles per hour in a windy chop without a drop of water touching you. It's a wonderful fishing machine . . . and at about 25 grand it should be!

Maybe it's sour grapes or plain old jealousy, but I'm offended by it. It just doesn't seem appropriate for fishing with its sleek design and creature comforts. He can fish the whole dusk bite and still make it in by dark, racing past me in perfect comfort while I'm getting drenched on a choppy evening, and he usually has several fish in the live well by the time I get there in the morning. I would be less than honest if I didn't admit that my resistance to these boats is weakening with each passing season. No doubt about it, they really are nice! Bear in mind, however, that you have to use a fairly powerful vehicle to tow a big bass rig, especially when trying to pull it out of the water on a steep launching ramp—a little four cylinder foreign car won't cut it. So, you're looking at another 25 thousand dollars for a 4x4 Suburban (or its equivalent). Most fly fishers with whom I am acquainted are professionals with above average incomes, yet they complain about spending 200 dollars for a float tube. But bass fishermen, who are mostly working people with ordinary incomes, readily assume a 50-thousand dollar obligation for these rigs! The latter, of course, will be on the lake nearly every weekend all year and most likely his family will also participate in the camping, boating and fishing. The typical fly fisher, on the other hand, will visit the lake only occasionally and his wife and children are rarely seen.

While they don't have the speed of a bass boat and don't handle well with a trolling motor, I think pontoon boats, sometimes called "party barges," have potential for fly fishers. Equipped with a 90-horse motor, a 24-foot model will go as fast as my boat and there is room for tubes, canoes, even jon boats. These awkward looking craft are equipped with comfortable seating, lots of storage, an ice box and even a barbe-cue. A removable canopy provides welcome shade, but also makes fly casting impossible from the boat itself. The advantage of a "houseboat" type of craft lies in the ability to transport a number of anglers and their gear to a desirable area of the lake where the boat can be moored as a kind of base camp. The tubing or wading angler can return to the boat to escape the sun, rest, eat lunch, get another rod or even tie a few flies whenever he wishes. Moreover, pontoon boats are comparatively inexpensive. They sell new for less than half the price of a fiberglass bass boat because the hull only amounts to two aluminum pontoons. They are normally sold with a 35-horse motor, but that's too small (slow) on a big lake. I used to make fun of the big motors, but, believe me, I grow weary of running hour after hour to get to the area I want to fish. If I buy a pontoon boat, and I'm giving some thought to it, I will order it with a 90-horse-power motor. I think it would make a great set-up for a guiding operation because most fly fishers would rather fish alone in their own personal water craft than to be carried around in a bass boat all day.

Whatever boat you buy, be sure it's large

enough to carry your float tube. There are times when you will want to moor the boat and fish from the tube—circumstances permitting. The float tube is quite impervious to the effects of any wind short of a gale, while it's nearly impossible to fly fish and handle a boat at the same time when the wind is blowing. I also want the tube available so I can access the kinds of backwater areas we discussed in Chapter 2. If you have enough room to transport it, a larger inflatable craft, such as Brooks Bouldin's Kikk Boat, is even better because it can be boarded directly from the main boat in deeper water. It is necessary to step out of the boat and stand on the bottom in order to get in and out of a float tube, but hard bottom may not be accessible on southern lakes. More than once I have stepped out of the boat only to plunge into water over my head!

If you are planning to buy a boat, you may want to look at a used ones. People often buy a boat on impulse, use it a few times, and then it sits in the garage for years until they tire of looking at it and sell it. One of our club members recently bought a 16-foot aluminum boat, completely equipped with a 20-horsepower Mercury motor, trailer, trolling motor and depth finder for $900. It had hardly been used at all. The paint wasn't even worn off the propeller. The same rig, new from a dealer, would cost at least $5,000.

Finally, those fly fishers who neither own nor wish to own a power boat need not despair. They can still fish choice areas of big lakes, in a limited way, if they will take the time to find access to the backwaters. There are usually dirt roads, built by government agencies and private interests, that access the lake in various locations. This approach will take some exploration and study, and may require permission from private land owners, but it is possible to get a vehicle to many of the same places that we go to by boat. One day last spring, I ran across Sam Rayburn reservoir to a favorite spot on the north shore. I was incredulous when I saw one of our club members fishing there in his float tube without a moored boat in sight, miles from the nearest public access. Where was his boat? How did he get here? He had found a dirt road into the area and his power boat was home in the garage. The road was posted but he took the trouble to find the owner and got permission to cross the property. Still, if you fish a big lake regularly, you will become a power-boat owner sooner or later.

## BOATMANSHIP

A large fresh water impoundment is an inland sea and a degree of boatmanship is required to operate on it efficiently and safely. Having spent my working life as an offshore charter boat captain, I vowed upon retirement that I would never acquire another power boat of any kind, with its inevitable maintenance problems and expenses. (Someone once defined a boat as a "hole in the water into which you pour money," and I can certainly attest to that.) The biggest pitfall is that you may find yourself going boating rather than fishing. It will certainly seem that way at first, when it's all new and strange, but the hassle of launching, trailering and maintaining the boat will become routine in a short while, like operating your car. It is highly desirable, if you can afford it, to keep the boat in a marina, so all you have to do is check the gas, push the starter and go fishing.

The competent boater is thoroughly familiar with the equipment, not only its operation, but also how to take care of it mechanically. You should be able to make minor repairs and have the tools to do so. In cluttered waters, it's a good idea to carry a spare propeller because it is very easy to destroy one on a stump or log. A couple of years ago, I did just that in a very remote area and breathed a sigh of relief that I had a spare prop. Unfortunately, although I had a crescent wrench that fit the big nut that holds the propeller in place, I did not have a pair of pliers to remove the cotter pin. I broke the forceps that I carry in my vest trying to get the pin out. After an hour's paddle, I found a bass fisherman who had a pair of needle-nose pliers.

Don't get into things that you don't understand. I once decided to *fix* the miniature fuel pump on the motor when it failed to start at the launching ramp. When I removed the last screw from the housing, I saw dozens of little splashes as tiny springs, all sorts of itty-bitty metal parts and various pieces of black plastic flew out of the pump and hit the water. I spent that day at the mechanic shop instead of bass fishing. Not surprisingly, the problem was not related to the fuel pump.

A prudent boater foresees possible difficulties, and heeds early warnings of trouble before problems occur. For example, don't head across a large expanse of open water with a motor that is misfiring. Keep your equipment in a good state of repair at all times. Know how to find your way around the lake when the visibility is restricted. The most blatantly negligent boatman I have ever seen was the young guide who took me pike fishing on a remote Alaska lake. We fished the lake, which was little more than a wide spot in a very large river, from a heavy wooden skiff powered by a badly misfiring outboard motor. The motor kept dying, coughing and sputtering a couple of hundred yards upstream from where the lake spilled into a dangerous rapids. I noticed there was no anchor or paddle in the boat; no way to avoid going over the rapids if the motor died. I pointed this out to the young man and insisted that we return immediately to shore.

## OPERATE SAFELY

If thunderheads appear to be building, stay close to the nearest bank and do not attempt to cross the lake during a storm. Pull into a sheltered place and wait until it's safe. If you do get caught in the short, nasty chop that accompanies a thunderstorm, slow down immediately and concentrate on riding it out rather than trying to reach the bank in panic. Such a storm can be very dangerous if the boat is not prudently handled. Most accidents occur as a result of excessive speed. Quarter the bow into the wind, using just enough throttle to maintain steerage or, as I prefer, put out a good anchor on a long line and ride it out "on the hook." Waves may break into the boat and it's a good idea carry a bucket for bailing (those electric bilge pumps don't move much water and may fail at a critical time). The boat probably won't actually sink, especially the newer ones, because they have styrofoam flotation built into them.

A life jacket for each person is required equipment in most states. I admit that I often don't wear one, but I could pay a very dear price for that if I hit a stump at high speed some day. Most motors

come with a snap-cord that is attached to the kill
switch on the motor. You snap the cord to your clothing so the motor is instantly killed if you are thrown
into the water. I do attach that cord whenever I
operate the boat. A driverless boat will usually go into
a circle and may run over you. It's also a good idea to
keep your running lights in working order, even if you
don't plan to operate after dark. Boating accidents are
usually caused by lack of common sense, especially
by running too fast for prevailing conditions. In my 25
years as a charter boat captain, I saw a lot of accidents
and excessive speed was responsible for the vast
majority of them.

# CHAPTER SEVEN

## BONA FIDE FLIES AND OTHER THINGS

My philosophical wall, that division that separates bass from other fly rod quarry, gets even higher when it comes to the contents of my fly boxes. Tying for bream and trout is fun. Tying for bass is work, and it's much less interesting. Bream are infinitely more discerning, even selective on occasion. Their diet consists primarily of insects and other small organisms that can be duplicated in a traditional way. The tying challenges that they present stems from the fact that, unlike bass, a bluegill closely examines everything it puts into its mouth. They respond to hatches in a trout-like way, and tying for them offers the same exciting opportunities as coldwater tying.

There are myriad food forms in the southern ecosystem that are fun to tie, but, because of the opportunistic behavior and dietary preferences of the largemouth bass, tying flies for them does not hold the same fascination. The thrill of tying a successful new bass pattern is tempered by the knowledge that the old fly would likely work as well at the same time and place as the new one. "Real" fly fishers find smaller sunfish infinitely more interesting, and it is understandable that the bluegill is in fact more popular with sophisticated anglers than the bass. There is no more of a relationship between these species, although they inhabit the same waters, than between a Pacific salmon at sea and a brook trout in a New England stream. Bass are very intelligent and present many angling challenges, but fancy fly tying is not one of them. As long as the fly resembles a living creature of any sort, you can't go wrong. A bass will eat virtually anything that appears to be alive and that will fit into his mouth. They'll try anything once! Even on the bass side of the wall, however, I still prefer to imitate actual food forms because I derive greater rewards from fly fishing if I have an actual organism in mind not only when fishing, but also while working at the vise. That's how I have managed, in some perverse way, to rationalize the use of soft plastic. However lacking in aesthetics these lures may be, they at least mimic actual organisms.

There is no scientific, pragmatic or philosophical reason why the bass fisher should deprive himself of the genuine joys of fly fishing—the pleasure of melding with nature, awareness of the whole ecosystem, understanding the life cycles of indigenous food forms, and addressing the feeding patterns of the prey, etc.. The rewards that we derive from our angling are directly proportional to the level of sophistication applied to it. It is quite true that if the largemouth behaved more like a trout or bluegill it would be more popular with fly fishers. The largemouth's opportunism, irregular feeding patterns and subsurface lethargy does indeed relegate it to a lesser status as fly-rod quarry. And properly so. I don't disagree with that assessment or even try to offer arguments to the contrary. Poor old Mr. Bigmouth really is something of a second-class citizen in the fly fishing community.

Second-class citizen or not, no other gamefish has the memory of a black bass. It never forgets the shape and color of something that has caused an injury. There is a great deal of research that documents the bass's elephantine memory. Fishing writer Chuck Tryon recently sent me some new research on the way bass react to baby turtles. Juvenile turtles have colorful undersides. A newly-hatched red-eared pond slider (*Chrysemys scripta elegans*), a common East Texas species, sports a bright yellow plastron (underside) with black spots and a solid olive back. I have seen bass take these little turtles, and tie a black-and-yellow bug to imitate them. The data that Chuck sent not only confirms my suspicions that bass eject the baby turtle without swallowing it, but the researchers also found that the fish do so only once! The turtle scratches and bites the bass and, the researchers found, usually kills the fish if it swallows the turtle. Once bitten in the mouth, the bass will never take a turtle again for the rest of its life. In fact, the researchers concluded that the bright plastron markings are actually a warning to predators—like the bands on a coral snake—and that only young, uneducated bass mouth them. In view of this information I will not continue to imitate turtles. (If you have a copy of *The Sunfishes*, ignore that part. It's outdated.)

This ability to recall a bad experience seems to function most effectively in regard to topwater food forms, and bass exercise less caution with subsurface lures. I have found that bass will repeatedly take the same bottom-crawling offering more frequently than a topwater bait; probably because the latter is an occasional treat while the former represent foods that are regularly eaten for survival. The "educated" fish can afford to avoid a questionable surface organism, but it has to eat baitfish, crawfish and salamanders to survive.

A given bug may find few takers in a pond that receives a lot of pressure from fly fishers, but the same fly may be deadly on another lake that is fished primarily with casting lures and vice versa. There are certain ponds that I never fish with topwater flies, in order to "save" them for visiting fly fishers. If I hammer a pond with bugs, divers and sliders the fish soon become educated and virtually impossible to catch with surface flies. Believe me, bass are fast learners and, for that reason, there are significant drawbacks to catch-and-release fishing.

Every season bass fishers on Lake Sam Rayburn, near my home, get excited about some new lure, or an old one they may have rediscovered, which is producing extraordinary catches. The bait will be hot for awhile, only to lose its effectiveness in time. Bass readily take something they haven't seen before, but, especially in this era of catch and release, they quickly learn to recognize it as a source of pain and danger. Because it represents important forage species, however, the plastic worm continues to repeatedly fool fish who learned long ago that topwater plugs and popping bugs are not food. It might seem at first thought that real fly fishing should produce good results on a crowded public lake where the bass may have never seen a hair bug. Unfortunately, such fish often learn to avoid all surface food forms, so they feed exclusively in the depths.

## TOPWATER BASS FLIES

There are three basic types of surface bass flies: bugs, sliders and divers. Using dyed deer body hair I tie each of them in four solid colors: black, olive, natural and cream. These are tied in just four sizes: 2/0, 2, 6, 8 (and, only in the case of the diver, size10). I rarely use the small, farm-pond sizes while seriously pursuing bass in larger waters. Ninety percent of my surface fishing is done with these basics.

The new warmwater fly tier goes through a phase in which he tries to tie every pattern he reads about. In time, when he learns that bass aren't trout and that fancy flies are not necessary to catch them, he settles into his own selection of basics. For bluegill fishing, which is my favorite angling pursuit, my fly boxes are (like the trout fisher's) crammed with all sorts of stuff that would take pages to list and describe. But when I head for the big lake looking only for serious bass fishing, and I don't anticipate unusual circumstances that may require special flies, my boxes contain the following basic selection:

### FLIES

Size 2/0 Chuggers - 4 natural, 2 black, 2 olive, 2 cream
Size 2   Chuggers - 4 natural, 2 black, 2 olive, 2 cream
Size 6   Chuggers - 6 natural, 4 black, 4 olive
Size 2/0 Divers     - 4 natural, 2 black, 2 olive, 2 cream
Size 6   Divers     - 4 natural, 4 black, 4 olive, 2 cream
Size 2   Grinnel   -12 natural, 4 black, 4 olive, 2 cream
Marabou Muddler - 6 white,   6 black, 6 olive, 6 brown
Plus one or two each of the Hairy Mouse Slider, Lester's Jointed Diver and maybe a couple of dragonfly and deer-hair sunfish patterns

### LURES

Soft Worm     - 12 pumpkinseed, 12 black, 12 olive
Soft Lizard    - 12 pumpkinseed, 12 black, 12 olive
Soft Crawfish - 12 green, 12 red
Worm Hooks - 24 Eagle Claw Lazer Point, size-1
Spinner Bait  -  2 white, 2 yellow, 2 black
Mini-Jig       -  6 white, 6 yellow, 6 black

Far and away the single most productive bass fly in my box is the Grinnel Fly, a natural rabbit-strip slider tied on a size 2 hook. There are times when I regret not having my trout and bream boxes on the big lake, but I don't normally carry light tackle in the bass boat anyway.

### HAIR BUGS

A hair bug can simulate a food item of some sort—a large terrestrial insect, a small mammal or bird, or (less likely) a frog—but it can also be fished as an attractor, appealing solely to the fish's territorial instincts. The difference is more in how it's fished rather than how it's tied. Many of my angling friends enjoy intricate fly tying and creating beautifully sculpted amphibians, rodents and reptiles with stacked deer hair of many colors. Fly tying is a wonderful hobby and we all enjoy getting creative once in awhile to fight boredom. I tie commercially and, believe me, tying the same thing over and over, day after day, takes all the fun out of it. It has been my experience, and you lazy tyers can rejoice in this, that solid color hair bugs fish better than banded or laterally stacked bodies. I don't stack hair at all anymore because it serves no practical purpose and I would rather spend the time on the lake than at the tying bench. I go through something like 300 bugs in a year's fishing and I can't possibly use a bug that takes two hours to tie.

I strongly recommend, however, whether you use multiple or solid colors, that you stay away from very bright hues and concentrate on the drabber tones that are more common in nature. I can't say that bass will hit a somber fly more readily than a vivid one (they will, after all, try anything once) but it's a fact that such gaudy patterns do not resemble anything regularly seen around these lakes. While an occasional handsome organism, such as the adult regal moth with its gorgeous orange-and-yellow markings, the mating chorus frog with its ornate dorsal of greens and yellows, or a chartreuse katydid does sometimes fall prey to an opportunistic bass, virtually everything the fish sees on the surface of the lake is some combination of brown, gray, dirty cream, black or olive tones.

Back in the Golden Age of bass bugging, it was debated whether fish could see color because scientists were unsure about how a fish's eyes worked. I think the current view is that they may not perceive color in the same way we do, but they can distinguish one color from another. So, colors are important in fly tying even if fish do perceive them only as shades of gray. Thank goodness! Fly tiers would have been utterly devastated if science concluded that fish cannot tell one color from another.

Every angler knows that confidence in a lure is more important than the lure itself, and I am confident that the following patterns will serve you well anywhere largemouth reside. You will also note that all of these patterns are more sparsely tied than usually seen these days. For example, one marabou blood feather is used instead of two, a single pair of hackles for the wing instead of the three or more pairs commonly used by many warmwater tiers, and a sparse hair-tip skirt is used instead of a bushy hackle. I find that sparser ties definitely fish better than heavily-dressed flies. Bass flies are often intentionally overdressed for purely aesthetic reasons and, while it may be good for the fly shop, too much material is counterproductive on the lake.

## TEXAS CHUGGER

NOTE: The fly tying sequences that follow are intended for tiers who have mastered the basics. If you are a newcomer to warmwater fly fishing and tying, free fly tying classes are offered by nearly all fly fishing clubs. Write to the Federation of Fly Fishers, P.O. Box 1595, Bozeman, Montana 59771 for the name and address of a chapter near you.

## TEXAS CHUGGER NATURAL

Hook:      Mustad 3366, size 2/0
Thread:    6/0 black and 3/0 black Monocord
Weedguard: Mason 25 lb. mono or other .019" stiff mono
Post:      Fox squirrel tail hair or brown calf tail
Tail:      Brown marabou
Wing:      Two cree or grizzly hackle feathers, splayed
Skirt:     Natural deer-body hair tips
Body:      Natural deer-body hair. White face optional
Eyes:      10mm white/black hollow doll eyes

## TEXAS CHUGGER BLACK

Hook:      Mustad 3366, size 2/0
Thread:    6/0 black and 3/0 black Monocord
Weedguard: Mason 25 lb. mono or other .019" stiff mono
Post:      Black calf tail
Tail:      Black marabou
Wing:      Grizzly hackle feathers, splayed
Skirt:     Black deer-body hair tips
Body:      Black deer-body hair. White face optional
Eyes:      10mm white/black hollow doll eyes

## TEXAS CHUGGER OLIVE

Hook:      Mustad 3366, size 2/0
Thread:    6/0 black and 3/0 black Monocord
Weedguard: Mason 25 lb. mono or other .019" stiff mono
Post:      Fox squirrel tail hair or olive calf tail
Tail:      Olive marabou
Wing:      Two cree or grizzly hackle feathers, splayed
Skirt:     Natural deer-body hair tips
Body:      Olive deer-body hair. White face optional
Eyes:      10mm yellow/black hollow doll eyes

## TEXAS CHUGGER CREAM

Hook:      Mustad 3366, size 2/0
Thread:    6/0 white and 3/0 white Monocord
Weedguard: Mason 25 lb. mono or other .019" stiff mono
Post:      Fox squirrel tail hair or tan calf tail
Tail:      Cream marabou
Wing:      Two cree or grizzly hackle tips, splayed
Skirt:     Cream deer-body hair tips
Body:      Cream deer-body hair.
Eyes:      10mm  white/black hollow doll eyes

### TYING SEQUENCES - TEXAS CHUGGER

STEP 1 - Crimp the barb and sharpen the hook

STEP 2 - Using 6/0 thread, attach the weedguard at a position opposite the hook point. Extend the windings about a third of the way down the bend. Wrap a short thread base immediately forward of the weedguard tie-in point. Cement these windings and let them dry.

STEP 3 - Select a clump of squirrel tail or kiptail for the post, even the tips, and attach the hair directly on top of the thread base. Use a minimal number of thread wraps. The length of the post should be equal to about half the length of the hook shank.

STEP 4 - Tie a full marabou feather directly on top of the post windings. Make the marabou about 1 1/2 times the shank length. Use minimal turns of thread.

STEP 5 - Select two matching hackle feathers from the same neck. Even the tips and clip the butts. The trimmed feathers should be twice the length of the hook shank. Do not trim or strip the barbules. Attach each feather separately, on either side of the existing windings, to form a splayed wing. Whip finish and cement. If you intend to trim the fly to a diving minnow configuration, you may want tie these hackles flat— face to face—rather than splayed.

STEP 6 - Attach 3/0 Monocord on the cemented windings. Select a sparse clump of deer hair for the skirt, even the tips, and place it directly on top of the same windings, making the length slightly shorter than the marabou. Take a couple of loose turns of thread to flatten the skirt down somewhat.

STEP 7 - Advance the thread to the bare shank ahead of the windings. Take a couple of half hitches on the bare shank to prevent heavy tail materials from rolling when you spin the hair. Spin several clumps of deer hair, working forward to the eye, leaving only enough room to attach the weedguard later. At this point, you can either trim the fly to a Dahlberg Diver configuration or continue to step 8 if you want a bug.

STEP 8 - Remove the fly from the vise and trim the bottom flat. Then, thoroughly coat the face of the bug with head cement until all the hair is lying flat. The head cement must be on the thick side or it won't lay the hair down. Let the fly dry overnight.

STEP 9 - The face should be about 3/4 inch wide. Clip the bottom as you would with any hair bug, but don't cut on a taper—go straight back. Then, following the scissor cuts you have just made, trim straight down the sides with the razor blade at right angles to the bottom. The body will now be square on three sides. The top of the bug is still untrimmed.

STEP 10 - Make an indentation with a wood burner or scissors, just large enough to receive the 10mm eyes at each front bottom corner of the partially-trimmed bug. Attach the eyes with Goop or 5-minute epoxy.

STEP 11 - When the eyes have dried, trim the top of the bug with a razor blade. Start just above the eyes and taper this cut toward the rear. Be careful not to cut the tail windings or the skirt. If the back is too high, the bug will float "belly up" when it gets saturated with water.

STEP 12 - Using curved scissors, round off all sharp corners on the back, face and sides of the bug. Smooth the body with a razor blade.

STEP 13 - Attach the weedguard and finish the head. Cement the thread windings. The fly is now ready to fish.

I have found the method of trimming the back after the eyes have been attached to be a lot easier. Also, the trimming job is easier if the untrimmed face is cemented first. Best of all, this fly can also become a diver by simply trimming it to that configuration after completing step 7. The diver simulates a baitfish and, when fished properly, is a better imitation of a small frog than a bug.

# A HAIR BUG FOR THE HARRIED TYER

*Tap's Bug*

Some time back in the 1940s, H.G. Tappley, then editor of *Outdoors Magazine*, introduced an incredibly basic, and quite effective, version of the hair bug. Further popularized by J. Edson Leonard, Tap's Bug is easily constructed in only a few minutes by anyone who knows the basics of spinning deer-body hair. After attaching the monofilament weedguard in the usual way, simply tie on a thick clump of bucktail, about the length of the hook shank, for the tail and spin successive clumps of hair to the eye. Trim the bottom flat and taper the sides and back as shown in the illustration. This bug (and possibly any other hair bug) will fish better if you trim it with scissors rather than a razor blade, leaving a rough, stubbly texture. I usually attach hollow doll eyes, although Tappley did not, to help with flotation and to stabilize the lure in the water.

This bug is rarely tied today because it just doesn't satisfy our aesthetic inclinations, but I can assure you that it will take as many bass as the fanciest creation from the vise of the most famous fly tier. As we have seen, pattern rarely matters in bass bugging. It's the action the angler imparts to the bug that counts, and an assortment of these basic bugs in several colors and sizes is all the practical angler needs. In fact, a simple Tap's Bug, tied with natural deer hair on a size 1/0 hook, will do the job anywhere, anytime. I recognize that there is more to fly tying than just catching fish, and reducing things to their basics, however pragmatic and effective, takes at least half the fun out of it. I believe my friend, Brooks

Bouldin, who says that only half of fly tying is for the fish. The other half is for our own gratification. How we divide our angling time between the vise and the lake is a matter of personal choice.

## WATER SNAKES AND RABBIT STRIPS

Topwater rabbit-strip sliders, like my Grinnel Fly, are completely reptilian and mimic snakes. Bass have great difficulty in resisting any sort of long, undulating, worm-like creature, whether tied with hair and presented on the surface, or molded with soft plastic and crawled along the bottom.

There are about 20 species of water snakes (*Natrix*) that a bass might see. They vary widely in color and an observant angler will want to identify common species on his home water. Mostly juveniles, which are less than a foot long, are taken by bass, but I have also seen bass grab snakes as long as 18 inches. The water snake commonly feeds and swims under water (I have seen them take crawfish off the bottom) so the Grinnel fly can also be dressed with solid eyes for use with a sink-tip line in shallow water. Strike detection is less of a problem when imitating a water snake, because these creatures, unlike salamanders, swim quite rapidly. As we have seen in preceding chapters, retrieving a subsurface fly rapidly allows the angler to feel the take and react accordingly.

There are also garter (*Thamnophis*) and ribbon (*Tropidoclonion*) snakes that are more or less aquatic. They are more brightly colored than the *Natrix* and present many interesting color modifications of the Grinnel Fly for the creative tyer. Juvenile garter snakes are smaller than the Natrix, only five or six inches long. Like the water snakes they are not venomous and are quite harmless.

In a typical year in Texas, ten people die from spider bites, four from lightning, over five hundred drown, four thousand are killed in automobile accidents and a grand total of five die from snake bites. You are as likely to be killed by lightning as by a snake! Those five were probably elderly or infirm, suffered from severe allergies or were very small children. Snakes present little danger to the warmwater angler.

# GRINNEL FLY

GRINNEL FLY
Hook:       Mustad 3366, 2/0, 2 and 6
Thread:     3/0 Monocord, black
Weedguard: .019 hard monofilament
Tail:       Thin, natural brown rabbit strip, about 4" long
Collar:     Natural deer-body hair tips
Body:       Natural deer-body hair
Eyes:       4mm doll eyes
Head:       3/0 black Monocord

This is, without doubt, the most effective bass fly in
my arsenal. I tie it in three colors. Natural works best
but black and olive follow closely behind, especially
on cloudy days.

## TYING SEQUENCES - GRINNEL FLY

STEP 1 - Crimp the barb and sharpen the hook.

STEP 2 - Tie in the weedguard at about the middle
of the shank, or a little forward of the middle. You
want a small head, so keep it well forward. Extend
the windings back about one-third down the bend
and return, making a small thread base just ahead of
the weedguard butt. Cement the thread and let it dry.

STEP 3 - Using a razor blade, cut a very narrow strip
from a tanned rabbit hide, following the natural
direction of the hair. The narrower the strip, the
easier the fly will cast. About 1/8" wide is good. Precut
strips are generally too wide and must be cut in half.

STEP 4 - Tie one end of the strip, on the thread base,

directly on top of the hook. Make sure the hair tips point rearward. Cement the thread wraps.

STEP 5 - Select a sparse bunch of deer hair and even the tips. You are going to spin a deer-body hair collar over the place where the rabbit-fur strip was secured. With the tips of the deer-body hair pointing rearward, take two loose turns of thread and spin the hair completely around the windings. It's difficult to spin hair on a thread base, so it may take a little practice. The secret is to use light thread tension. The tips should not extend past the bend of the hook. Take several loose thread wraps to lay the collar down.

STEP 6 - Spin and pack several more bunches of hair to the hook eye, leaving only enough room to tie off the weedguard. Remove the fly from the vise.

STEP 7 - Using scissors, rough cut the body to a slender, torpedo shape. Finish trimming with sharp razor blade.

STEP 8 - Return the fly to the vise. Tie off the weedguard, whip finish and cement.

STEP 9 - Make indentations with a wood burner or scissors to accept 4mm doll eyes. Place the eyes far forward, near the eye of the hook, and cement them with Goop or epoxy. Either hollow or solid eyes can be used, depending upon the amount of buoyancy desired. The eyes of a water snake are very inconspicuous, but I use them on this fly to regulate buoyancy. For a slow-sinking version, use solid eyes.

Neutral buoyancy can easily be achieved by trimming and by the type of eyes selected. The fly should be slightly buoyant so it will ride low in the surface film when fished topwater, and it should be tied with neutral buoyancy when fished near the bottom on a sinking line. I tie this fly in various colors, but the above pattern is by far the most productive in my waters. This fly looks so realistic slithering through the weeds, you'll have to resist the urge to eat it yourself.

## HAIRY MOUSE SLIDER

This slider, originated by Bill Lambing of Lufkin.
Texas, is my favorite "mouse" imitation. While less
aesthetic than many of the cute little mice that are
seen in catalogs (this one is downright ugly in fact)
this is one of the few topwater patterns that readily
entices a bass waiting in ambush. For some inexplicable reason, the Hairy Mouse Slider seems to work
better than other topwater offerings in the cool
conditions of early spring and late fall. I have even
caught bass on this in the dead of winter, which isn't
all that dead in East Texas. Mice and other small
mammals can swim, and this fly works best with a
fairly fast retrieve. Bill also fishes it on a sinking line.

### HAIRY MOUSE SLIDER
Hook:    Mustad 37189, heavy-wire stinger shape, size 10
Thread:  Monocord, size A, black
Weedguard: Stiff monofilament. (The original fly does not
           use a weedguard.)
Tail:      Chamois strip, about eight inches long, cut very
           narrow
Skirt:     Long, natural deer-hair tips
Body:    Natural deer hair, spun and clipped
Head:    Tying thread

## TYING SEQUENCE

STEP 1 - Attach a weedguard if desired.

STEP 2 - Tie in a chamois strip, about eight inches long, at a point opposite the barb.

STEP 3 - Select a clump of long, natural deer hair. Even the tips and stack it directly on top of the tail windings. The tips should extend back about a half a shank length or more. Do not flair the hair more than necessary. Advance the thread forward and make a short thread base to stack the next clump. Do not trim the butts. They stay in the fly—I told you it was ugly.

STEP 4 - Select another clump of hair, even the tips, and stack it on the thread base directly in front of the first clump. This clump should be shorter than the first one to give the untrimmed back a tapered look. Gently pack the hair and add a drop of cement.

STEP 5 - Spin successive clumps (you can trim off the tips on these) to the hook eye, leaving enough room to tie off the weedguard and finish the head.

STEP 6 - Using only scissors for an intentionally rough look, trim the bottom to a rounded, oval shape, leaving only enough gape for the hook to function.

STEP 7 - Using only scissors, no razor blade, clip the sides and top at a thirty degree angle, from the eye upward. The result will be a ragged, rather unattractive fly that seems out of proportion on the small stinger hook. This is done to maximize the natural texture and reduce rejection by cautious bass. Some recent versions of this fly have been tidied up to improve appearances, but I have better success fishing the scruffy original.

## MARABOU MUDDLER

Every fly fisher has a special fly they just know will do the job when all else fails. Mine is the Marabou Muddler. This is the design I use for all of my standard streamers, varying the color accordingly. I have seen this fly tied with a huge deer-hair head and a lot of fluffy dressing that makes it float on top of the water like a bug. That is not the version. My idea of a Marabou Muddler is that presented by Terry Hellekson, in his book *Popular Fly Patterns*. When properly tied, these flies neither sink nor float; they are neutrally buoyant. Depth, if desired, is achieved with a sinking line, leader or split shot, not by tying lead into the fly which spoils its action. With a number of colors in sizes 6 to 10, I can effectively represent all of the fifty-plus species of baitfish that occur in my part of the Lone Star state. The following patterns are from his book and they were recently reprinted in *American Angler* as well.

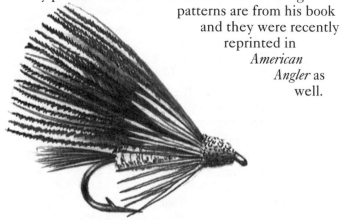

## MARABOU MUDDLER BLACK
Hook:     Mustad 9672, sizes 4 to10
Thread:   Black
Tail:     Crimson red hackle fibers, tied short
Body:     Silver tinsel chenille or other synthetic material
Wing:     Black marabou over gray squirrel tail
Topping:  Six strands of peacock herl
Collar:   Natural deer-hair tips
Head:     Natural deer-body hair

## MARABOU MUDDLER BROWN
Hook:     Mustad 9672, sizes 4-10
Thread:   Brown
Tail:     Crimson red hackle fibers, tied short

Body:      Gold tinsel chenille or other synthetic material
Wing:      Brown marabou over yellow calf tail
Topping:  Six strands of peacock herl
Collar:    Natural deer-hair tips
Head:      Natural deer-body hair

## MARABOU MUDDLER GRAY
Hook:      Mustad 9672, sizes 4 to10
Thread:    Gray
Tail:      Crimson red hackle fibers, tied short
Body:      Silver tinsel chenille or other synthetic material
Wing:      Gray marabou over gray squirrel tail
Topping:  Six strands of peacock herl
Collar:    Natural deer-hair tips
Head:      Natural deer-body hair

## MARABOU MUDDLER OLIVE
Hook:      Mustad 9672, sizes 4 to10
Thread:    Brown
Tail:      Crimson red hackle fibers, tied short
Body:      Gold tinsel chenille or other synthetic material
Wing:      Olive marabou over fox squirrel tail
Topping:  Six strands of peacock herl
Collar:    Dyed brown deer-hair tips
Head:      Dyed brown deer-body hair

## MARABOU MUDDLER YELLOW
Hook:      Mustad 9672, sizes 4 to10
Thread:    Brown
Tail:      Crimson red hackle fibers, tied short
Body:      Gold tinsel chenille or other synthetic material
Wing:      Yellow marabou over brown calf tail
Topping:  Six strands of peacock herl
Collar:    Dyed brown deer hair tips
Head:      Dyed brown deer body hair

## MARABOU MUDDLER WHITE
Hook:      Mustad 9672, sizes 4 to10
Thread:    White
Tail:      Crimson red hackle fibers, tied short
Body:      Silver tinsel chenille or other synthetic material
Wing:      White marabou over gray squirrel tail
Topping:  Six strands of peacock herl
Collar:    Tannish gray deer-hair tips
Head:      White deer-body hair

## LESTER'S JOINTED DIVER

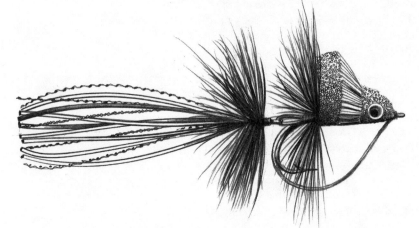

Lester Lehman, formerly with the Angler's Edge fly shop in Houston, Texas, is now a saltwater guide and a superb warmwater angler. His Jointed Diver, inspired by Jim Stewart's Jointed Popper, is a real bass getter. This is a big-fish fly. It looks much larger in the water than it really is and often entices a lurking lunker that ignores everything else. It's especially effective on fish that are observed basking in the shallows, often making a spinner bait unnecessary.

## LESTER'S JOINTED DIVER
Hook:       Tiemco #8089, size 2
Thread:     3/0 Monocord brown (Lester uses flat nylon
                and Kevlar)
Weedguard: .019 hard Mason mono
Hackle:     Soft, webby butt hackles, 2 green and 1 brown
Skirt:      Olive deer-body hair tips
Collar:     Olive deer-body hair
Body:       Olive deer-body hair
Trailer:    Mustad 3366, size 2
                10 strands of medium rubber hackle, purple
                10 strands of medium rubber hackle, orange
                10 strands each of black, silver and green
                    Crystal Flash
                3 soft and webby green butt hackles

STEP 1 - Place the 3366 trailer hook in the vise. Starting at the eye, wrap a thread base back to the middle of the shank.

STEP 2 - Tie-in 10 strands of purple rubber hackle, about 3 inches long, at a point directly behind the end of the thread base. Tie-in the orange rubber hackle on top of these windings. On top of the same windings add the green, black and silver Crystal Flash.

STEP 3 - Directly ahead of those windings, tie in one soft, green butt hackle. Wrap it forward on the original thread base so it covers about a third of that thread base. Tie in another butt hackle and wrap it forward, followed by a third hackle to fill the hook to the eye. Whip finish and cement.

STEP 4 - Remove the finished trailer from vise and cut the hook off with wire cutters directly behind the tail windings. Leave a small stub, about 1/8 inch.

STEP 5 - Insert the Tiemco 8089 hook in the vise.

STEP 6 - Starting at a point opposite the hook point, attach the weedguard material. Then tie in another section of monofilament on top of the weedguard windings. Run that section of mono through the eye of the trailer hook so the rubber legs ride on top and the Crystal Flash is on the bottom. Bring the end of that mono attachment section back to the shank of the main hook, forming a small loop. Lash that loop down tightly and firmly. The trailer is now attached. Be sure the loop allows the trailer to swing freely.

STEP 7 - Attach a large, soft green butt hackle and wind it forward, keeping the wraps close and tight. Then add a brown hackle and follow that with another green butt hackle. Keep these fairly tight so you don't run out of shank later. After winding the three hackles, you should have at least 3/4 of an inch of bare shank remaining. Temporarily tie back the hackles with a couple of turns of soft lead wire.

STEP 8 - Spin the first clump of deer hair with tips left on and facing to the rear. These tips will form the skirt. Spin successive clumps of hair to the eye. Lester uses white deer hair for the final clump.

STEP 9 - Remove the fly from vise and trim the body to a Dahlberg Diver configuration. Lester trims the head small and the collar quite thick. Remove the lead wire from the hackles.

STEP 10 - Cut or burn an indentation on each side of the head, and affix 4mm doll eyes. Lester uses one yellow and one white eye, on the theory that if the bass rejects the white eye fly, it might like the yellow eye better when Lester casts the fly again to the other side of the fish.

STEP 11 - Attach the weedguard. Whip finish and cement.

### MORE ABOUT SOFT PLASTIC
### AND OTHER LURES

For a worm-type bait, I like the four-inch Augertail, made by the Mann Bait Company of Eufaula, Alabama. It is very light and castable because most of the body consists of a long, thin tail that bass find irresistible. Unfortunately the small Augertail is hard to find in stores. The Bass Pro Shop's Sidewinder is also a good choice, as is Renegade's four-inch Twirltail.

My favorite water dog imitation is a small pumpkinseed "lizard" from the Zoom Bait Company. It is tan with black spots and looks just like the real thing. Remember, just looking like the organism is not enough—the texture is the key. The two-inch, green Soft Craw Jr., also from Renegade, rounds out my "worm" box. These baits don't last very long and must be replaced after one or two fish (discard them with care—they are not biodegradable and many animals will eat them). They cost about a quarter each and I use several in an hour's fishing. Some brands are more durable than others but also tend to be heavier. There are many colors available but I only carry black, pumpkinseed and olive (or "motor oil" in bassin' parlance). Kits and materials are available to pour your own baits in exactly the density and colors that you want. I intend to get into this in the future. If I make them myself it might take some of the sting out of the whole thing. If I can find a way to mold the polymer directly onto the hook, maybe can I stick a couple of feathers in it and call it a fly!

I would think that one of the manufacturers might make some special baits for the fly rod if there were any market for them. Right now there's a market of three: me and two friends! There are also many kinds of hooks on the market, each claiming to be superior. They all have either offset shanks or special barbs on the shank to hold the bait in place. I am sold on the Eagle Claw Lazer Point, size-1, which has a straight shank with two barbs behind the eye. Size-1 is the smallest I have found and it's perfect for the four-inch worm. It should be rigged so the lure rides straight. Rather than describe how to do that, I suggest that you simply ask any knowledgeable bass fisherman to show you. Tom Nixon recommends pegging it with a toothpick to help hold it on the hook while casting, but I haven't had any trouble with it coming off, just rig it "Texas style." (Again, Tom wrote that a long time ago and both hooks and poly-mers have improved since then.) The hook point must be razor sharp because it's embedded in the bait. (That's what makes it so wonderfully weedless.)

While I am admittedly lazy about sharpening hooks, I do sharpen these. Believe it or not, you can crimp the barb as long as you check it frequently to make sure it's still properly rigged and if you use a new, intact bait. Crimping the main barb is very advantageous because it helps drive the hook point home and also allows a much cleaner release of the occasional gullet-hooked fish.

Never fish with a soft plastic lure unless you have a pair of needle nose pliers (forceps aren't strong enough to do the job). If you leave the barb in place, you will also need angular wire cutters to facilitate the release of a deeply-hooked fish. I have a pair of these cutters in the boat and I can reach down into the fish's throat, clip off the barb and back the hook out cleanly. This is not a major problem on a floating or sink tip line but, just one more time, heavy sinking lines are definitely a "no no," at least on the heavily-vegetated, muddy-bottom lakes that I fish. If you fish the lure properly, you won't have too many problems of this nature, but it's a good idea to be prepared.

You can make your own spinner baits from the detailed instructions in Tom Nixon's book, or Ron Knight offers them for sale (3555 Tudor Drive,

Leavenworth, KS 66048). Ron's baits are of high quality and are designed for the fly rod. You can also purchase tiny spinner baits at discount stores and tackle shops. All of these are made for ultra-light spinning and they are marketed under brand names like Mr. Twister, Beetle Spin, H&H and others. They usually come with a 1/16-ounce jig, which is too heavy to cast. Simply remove this and attach a 1/64-ounce mini-jig, dressed in whatever color marabou you choose. This is very important: you will find that the jig can go on the clip in either of two ways, depending upon whether you insert the wire in the left or right side of the hook eye. The jig must ride upside down, with the hook in the direction of the blade. Don't forget that!

You can also lighten the heavier jig that comes on the lure by filing the sides of the lead head (another Tom Nixon idea), or you can attach a weighted streamer of some sort, as long as it rides upside down and is tied on a ring-eye hook. Some commercial spinner baits come with the jig molded onto the wire and can only be modified with a file. Shop carefully. Ten-weight tackle will handle a 1/32-ounce jig, but that's maximum for any realistic fly rod application.

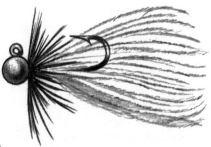

MINI-JIG
Hook:    1/64-ounce jig head, preformed. Paint and eyes
         optional
Wing:    Single marabou blood feather, white, black or
         yellow, about twice the length of hook shank,
         including the jig head.
Hackle:  Wound soft hackle, red or black

This is so incredibly easy to tie that no further explanation is required.

I still tie only the single monofilament weedguard. Some expert bass tyers use a double mono guard, which makes the fly almost completely weedless. Bear in mind, however, that as you increase the efficiency of the weedguard, you also decrease the efficiency of the hook. Tom Nixon uses a lot of wire in his fly tying, and his stirrup guard, based on the old "Snagless Sally" design, is probably the best of all weed guards. Why don't I use it? I must confess that I just haven't learned to tie it. Plain old laziness is the only excuse. I highly recommend the stirrup guard, and you can get the wire and instructions from Ron Knight. Ron sent me the wire several years ago and it's still sitting in a drawer.

# POSTSCRIPT

Largemouth bass are only vulnerable to "real" fly fishing part of the time; unfortunately, much less frequently than we would prefer. The bigger the water, the less likely that Mr. Bigmouth will respond to our necessarily shallow-running flies, and we have explored alternative ways to use the fly rod for lethargic, stillwater bass. The situation on these large reservoirs is analogous to that on a private spring creek where educated trout can only be induced to take a dry fly during a hatch. Bass likewise tend to rise to the bug or diver primarily during active feeding periods or under optimum conditions. Unlike the private stream, where only tiny dries may be permitted, the warmwater angler has many options that he can implement without compromising his conservation ethic. Only an attitude adjustment is required; an adjustment made easier by the knowledge that respected fly fishers of an earlier era had no qualms about drawing a dichotomy between bass and trout. These anglers unabashedly used all sorts of lures, even live bait, on a bass lake.

The years since Tom Nixon wrote his book have seen the development of megabucks tournaments, the proliferation of high-powered bass boats and the evolution of a bass-fishing genre. The plastic worm has become a symbol of the bassin' culture that real fly fishers detest, and I share those sentiments to an extent. Obviously I would prefer to fish with the flies that I tie, but the reality is, bluntly put, that at times they don't work very well. Soft plastic, however objectionable it may be, does work. It's as simple as that. This is essentially lure fishing and no *real* fly fisher would stoop to that level. It is admittedly a major transgression from traditional values. Soft plastic is not my first choice, but my philosophical wall allows me to rationalize its use. Besides, I like to catch bass on the fly rod and this is the best way to do it. My critics, and I am sure there will be many, can make a good case with their subjective arguments, but if they had spent as much time on the lake struggling with sinking lines and ineffective flies as I have, watching the bass fishermen ravage the fish, they might also be willing to explore new, nontraditional approaches.

The most virulent criticism will likely come from idealistic fly fishers who are still living in a fantasy world as far as largemouth bass are concerned. Trout fishers generally are more realistic about the fly fishing limitations of stillwater bass, and, although few will rush down to Kmart to buy a bag of worms, they will accept my conclusions more easily than my warmwater brethren. The latter will doubtless view this book as heretical, tasteless and low class. Such criticisms are clearly valid, to a point, but I will not accept charges directed at my sportsmanship or conservation principles. There's no moral issue here if sensible practices are followed. As long as the fly line isn't too heavy to transfer the initial strike to the line hand, so the hook can be set before the fish swallows the bait, the matter of ethics does not enter into the discussion. The only valid objections are strictly aesthetic. As the Scottish gille said to the American who wanted to fish with a nymph, "it's not a question of sportsmanship, old chap, it's a matter of good taste." Well, old chap, common sense is always in good taste. When properly handled on a floating line, soft plastic doesn't hurt the fish a bit. It's tremendously effective and takes more skill than you may realize. This can best be described as a kind of "hybrid" system that is neither bass fishing nor fly fishing but one that combines the best, (or in the opinion of some, the worst) elements of both. I present it because it is harmless if done right—and great fun.

# BIBLIOGRAPHY

Bergman, Ray. 1942. *Fresh Water Bass*. New York: Alfred A. Knopf.

_____. 1947. *With Fly, Plug and Bait*. New York: Wm. Morrow and Co.

Borger, Gary. 1991. *Designing Trout Flies*. Wausau, Wis.: Tomorrow River Press.

Brooks, Joe. 1947. *Bass Bug Fishing*. New York: A.S. Barnes & Co.

Conant, Roger. 1975. *A Field Guide to the Reptiles and Amphibians of Eastern and Central North America*. Boston: Houghton Mifflin.

Dalyrmple, Byron. 1972. *Modern Book of the Black Bass*. New York: Winchester Press.

Drury, Clyde E. 1979. *Book of the Black Bass*. Tacoma, Wash.: Clyde E. Drury.

Gallagher, Wallace W. 1937. *Black Bass Lore*. New York: G. Putnam's Sons.

Gasque, Jim. 1946. *Bass Fishing*. New York: Alfred A. Knopf.

Gordon, Sid M. 1955. *How to Fish From Top to Bottom*. Harrisburg, Pa.: Stackpole Co.

Gresham, Grits. 1966. *Complete Book of Bass Fishing*. New York: Harper and Row.

Harris, William C.. 1905. *The Basses—Fresh Water and Marine*. New York: Frederick A. Stokes.

Hellekson, Terry. 1979. *Practical Fly Patterns*. Salt Lake City: Peregrine Smith.

Henshall, James A. 1881. *Book of the Black Bass*. Cincinnati: Robert Clarke and Co.

_____. 1920. *Bass, Pike, Perch and Other Game Fishes of America*. Cincinnati: Stewart and Kidd Co.

Hollis, Harold C. 1945. *Bass Tackle and Tactics*. New York: A.S. Barnes.

Janes, Edward C., ed. 1970. *Fishing With Ray Bergman*. New York: Alfred A. Knopf.

Jones, Sheridan R. 1927. *Black Bass and Bass Craft*. New York: Macmillan Company.

Keith, Tom. 1989. *Flytying and Fishing for Panfish and Bass*. Portland, Oreg.: Frank Amato.

Knight, John Alden. 1942. *Moon Up, Moon Down*. New York: Charles Scribner's Sons.

_____. 1949. *Black Bass*. New York: G.P. Putnam's Sons.

Lincoln, Robert Page. 1952. *Black Bass Fishing*. Harrisburg, Pa.: Stackpole Company.

Livingston, A.D. 1974. *Fishing for Bass*. Philadelphia: J.B. Lippincott & Co.

Loudon, W.J. 1910. *The Small-Mouthed Bass*. Toronto: Hunter-Rose Co.

Lucas, Jason. 1947. *Lucas on Bass Fishing*. New York: Robert M. McBride and Co.

McCarthy, Eugene. 1900. *Familiar Fish*. New York: D. Appleton and Co.

McClane, A.J..1986. *Angling World*. New York: E.P. Dutton.

_____. 1974. *Field Guide to the Fresh Water Fishes of North America*. New York: Holt, Rhinehart and Winston.

McNally, Tom. 1978. *Flyfishing*. New York: Harper and Row

Nixon, Tom. [1968] 1977. *Fly Tying and Fly Fishing for Bass and Panfish*. New York: A.S. Barnes & Co.

Ripley, Ozark. 1924. *Bass and Bass Fishing*. Cincinnati: Sportsman's Digest Publishing.

Sosin, Mark and Bill Dance. 1974. *Practical Black Bass Fishing*. New York: Crown Publishers.

Stewart, Dick. 1989. *Bass Flies*. North Conway, N.H.: Northland Press.

_____ and Farrow Allen. 1992. *Flies for Bass and Panfish*. Intervale, N.H.: Northland Press.

Taylor, Rick. 1979. *Guide to Successful Bass Fishing*. Missoula, Mont.: Mountain Press.

Waterman, Charles. 1993. *Black Bass and the Fly Rod*. Harrisburg, Pa.: Stackpole.

_____. 1989. *Fly Rodding for Bass*. New York: Nick Lyons Books.

Weiss, John. 1976. *Advanced Bass Fishing*. New York: E.P. Dutton and Co.

Whitlock, Dave. 1988. *LL Bean Fly Fishing for Bass Handbook*. New York: Nick Lyons Books.